Praise for *Bare Minimum*

"A painfully honest and hilarious parenting book for us non-parenting-book-reading underachievers trying to survive the whole parenting experience. You know, I really could have used this book before my kids drove me insane. Next time write faster, James."

—Brian Gordon, creator of the webcomic *Fowl Language*

"James Breakwell's *Bare Minimum Parenting: The Ultimate Guide to Not Quite Ruining Your Child* is a witty and refreshing take on parenting in a modern world. I have always enjoyed following James' parental trials and tribulations on social media, and it's fun to seeing his musings come to life in this essential handbook!"

—Rebecca Mader, actress in *Once Upon a Time* and *Lost*

"I've never felt so guilt-free ignoring my child to read a book."

**—Laura Perlongo, Shorty Award–winning
cohost of the web series *We Need to Talk* and
guest commentator on MTV's *Catfish***

"Breakwell has a hit . . . uproariously funny and, at times, unexpectedly poignant."

**— Liliana Hart, *New York Times*
bestselling author and mom of five**

"Oh, parents! Read this book and free yourself from the blood sport that parenting has become! With humor, insight, and honesty, smart-ass James Breakwell tells you what no other parenting book has the guts to say: relax. You and the kids will be just fine."

—Kristan Higgins, *New York Times* bestselling author

"James Breakwell's *Bare Minimum Parenting* is a rollicking, entertaining manifesto for the half-assed revolution. Reading it was WAY more fun than writing my own books and raising my own kids."

—Carolyn Parkhurst, *New York Times* bestselling author of *The Dogs of Babel* and *Harmony*

"As a father of three children ages 25, 17, and 3, who are all reasonably well adjusted and jail-free, James Breakwell's views on kids and parenting speak to my soul. This book brings balance to the 300,000 misguided 'how to raise the perfect child' books out there that increase our stress level, as if answering 500 why questions from a toddler every day weren't stressful enough! If you have a kid, are planning on having a kid, or have friends who have kids and want to hold on to some of your sanity, this book is a must-read!"

—Jaime Casap, chief education evangelist at Google and free range parent

"I don't have any kids, and still I loved this book. I laughed and laughed, and then I reached the part about raising a child in your thirties or forties and I cried."

—David Litt, former speechwriter for President Obama and bestselling author of *Thanks, Obama*

"A parenting book like no other. Wise, hilarious, and a must-read for harassed, guilt-ridden parents everywhere. Parenting doesn't have to be high maintenance. Don't believe me? Read this."

—Vicki Psarias, bestselling author of *Mumboss* and founder of Honestmum.com

BARE MINIMUM

~~Superior~~

Parenting

BARE MINIMUM

~~Superior~~

Parenting

The Ultimate Guide to
Not Quite Ruining Your Child

James Breakwell

BenBella Books, Inc.

Dallas, TX

BenBella
BenBella Books, Inc.
10440 N. Central Expressway, Suite 800
Dallas, TX 75231
www.benbellabooks.com
Send feedback to feedback@benbellabooks.com

Printed in the United States of America
10 9 8 7 6 5 4 3 2

Library of Congress Cataloging-in-Publication Data
Names: Breakwell, James, author.
Title: Bare minimum parenting : the ultimate guide to not quite ruining your child / James Breakwell.
Description: Dallas, TX : BenBella Books, [2018] | Includes bibliographical references and index.
Identifiers: LCCN 2018020574 (print) | LCCN 2018021973 (ebook) | ISBN 9781946885623 (electronic) | ISBN 9781946885326 (trade paper : alk. paper)
Subjects: LCSH: Parenting. | Child rearing. | Parent and child.
Classification: LCC HQ755.8 (ebook) | LCC HQ755.8 .B7334 2018 (print) | DDC 649/.1—dc23
LC record available at https://lccn.loc.gov/2018020574

Editing by Leah Wilson
Copyediting by James Fraleigh
Proofreading by Lisa Story and Michael Fedison
Cover design by Ty Nowicki
Text design and composition by Aaron Edmiston
Author photo by David Van Deman
Printed by Lake Book Manufacturing

Distributed to the trade by Two Rivers Distribution, an Ingram brand
www.tworiversdistribution.com

Special discounts for bulk sales (minimum of 25 copies) are available.
Please contact bulkorders@benbellabooks.com.

To my wife and kids,
for always giving me something to write about.
Even when you shouldn't.

To my parents, for making me the person I am
today. I'm not sure if that's a compliment or
an insult.

Contents

Chapter 1

A Call to ~~Action~~
Inaction

Facts. Figures. Hard evidence. Peer-reviewed studies.

None of those things are in this book. This is a book about kids. Science is as powerless to explain them as it is to make you friends or get you laid. After studying children for generations, all that scientists know for sure is that scientists won't know anything for sure unless they get more grant money. And maybe tenure.

This lack of empirical data hasn't stopped countless "experts" from writing libraries of books on the right and wrong ways to raise a child. Their aim is to make you a better parent so you can make better kids who in turn make the world a better place.

Pass.

Why work harder to be a great parent when your kid will turn out just as well if you're a mediocre one? As for making the world a better place, the sun will swallow the earth in a mere five billion years. It's a waste of time to fix up temporary housing.

The world doesn't need another guide for raising children. In fact, it doesn't need another book of any kind. Reading can lead to eyestrain, headaches, and even war. Guess who made the best-seller list before he invaded Poland.

Clearly there's nothing more unethical than writing a parenting book. But people pay money for them, so I wrote one anyway. Trust me, no one is more disappointed in me than me. Except maybe my parents.

In my defense, this isn't really a book. Despite all the evidence to the contrary—it looks like a book, it smells like a book, and I called it a book literally four sentences ago—it's actually an *un*book. It exists solely to counteract the countless parenting books already in print. If those authors stopped publishing bad advice, I'd gladly abandon my unbook as well. But I made some phone calls, and none of the other writers agreed to give up their careers just because I asked them to. I guess I'll have to write this unbook after all. There goes my weekend.

Here's the tricky part: I've never actually read any of those other parenting books. All I know is that people who buy them go online and blame "underachieving" parents like me for ruining kids today. That's pretty much the only thing the internet is good for. Well, the only thing it's good for that doesn't lead to you clearing your browser history.

I get where those other parents are coming from. If I were them, I'd hate me, too. I'm doing everything wrong, yet the universe hasn't struck me down. My kids are on track to be self-sufficient adults all the same. Maybe my parenting approach works just as well as the overachieving one, but with less effort on my part. That sounds like the kind of thing other people might want to know about. I should write it down—and sell it for a modest but fair profit. Operators are standing by.

How the Children of Different Kinds of Parents Turn Out

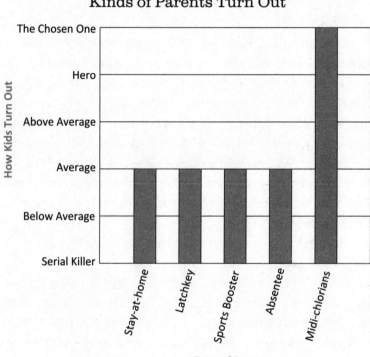

You made the smartest decision of your life just by picking up this book (and, yes, I'm calling it a book again; typing two extra letters was exhausting). You see, this isn't a book about overachieving as a parent. This isn't even a book about achieving exactly the right amount. This is a book about doing as little as possible without quite ruining your child. The goal of bare minimum parenting is to turn your kid into a functional adult using only a fraction of the effort spent by overachieving parents. Your kid will be just as good as their kids—if not better. Often, the easiest approach for you is also the best approach for your child. But if it's not, be lazy anyway. It's good to be consistent.

Overparenting is killing kids today. Well, not literally—although I wouldn't put anything past health-food nuts. No one knows the long-term effects of kale. Many overachieving moms and dads assume the harder they work, the better their kids will turn out, but the evidence doesn't bear that out. In fact, most parents who do too much raise a child who amounts to too little. Those are the cases I'll focus on, not because they're statistically relevant, but because they prove my point. Just don't accuse me of cherry-picking my data. Like my kids, I'll die before I touch fruit.

And, yes, you really do need this book to tell you how to do as little as possible. To avoid overparenting, you can't simply underparent. You must be strategically lazy. Many times, the course that takes the least effort today will create huge amounts of work down the road. This book is meant to save you time and energy overall. Parenting is all about the long game. It has to be. Kids grow up too damn slow.

Guilt by Association

If you're a parent, your guilt response is already kicking in. You feel terrible just for reading this far. What self-respecting parent would admit they DON'T want to work hard for their kid?

A wise one, that's who. There's no reason to feel bad about making something as easy as possible. Do you feel guilty when you solve a math problem with a calculator instead of an abacus? Do you consider yourself a failure if you use a shopping cart instead of holding thirty-five different items in your bare hands? Are you tormented by inner turmoil when you fly across the country rather than walking the whole way?

Of course not.

The only thing using a calculator or a shopping cart or an airplane makes you guilty of is being human. We're not the fastest or strongest creatures on earth, but we are the smartest. Our survival as a species depends on thinking up ways to make life easier. The prize for doing things the hard way isn't self-satisfaction. It's extinction.

Bare minimum parenting is just another tool. Sure, there are other, more effort-intensive ways to bring up a kid, but those are just more difficult means of arriving at the same end. Raising your child the hard way doesn't make you a better parent, just a less evolved one. Why start a fire by rubbing two sticks together when you could use a flamethrower? Time for s'mores.

Citation Needed

Why am I qualified to give you this advice?

The short answer is I'm not. The longer, more nuanced answer is I'm really, really not. That's why you should trust me completely.

I don't have a degree in elementary education, child psychology, or early childhood development. I majored in English, which only makes me an expert at making bad choices. No wonder I'm a parent.

I do have four kids age eight and under, although that doesn't make me a childcare expert, either. I might have some credibility if I'd already raised successful children, but all of mine are still too young for me to tell how they'll turn out. For all I know, they could become astronauts or bank robbers. Maybe they'll be both. Now I hope that happens. *Thieves in High Orbit* sounds like a better book than *Bare Minimum Parenting*.

Unfortunately, I can't wait around for the world's first space heist. If I raised my kids first and wrote a book afterward, I'd be an expert on children but a fraud on slacking off. You couldn't believe a word I said. Instead, you should believe me unconditionally because I'm not believable at all.

How Much You Should Trust a Parenting "Expert"

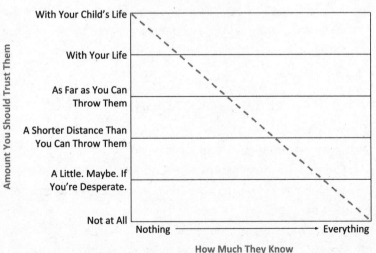

All Downhill from Here

The time to stop trying is now. The fact that you're reading this book at all suggests you're already working too hard. Don't put it down, though. You're exactly the kind of person who needs it.

Over the course of this book, I'll teach you to get by while doing less. If you do it right, you'll out-parent overachieving moms and dads without putting in much effort at all. Some might call that laziness; I call it efficiency. Don't worry, the lesson will stick. I'll beat that dead horse until it's glue. Clear your schedule. We have a lot of nothing to do.

Chapter 2
Your Child Is
~~One of a Kind~~
Uniquely Unoriginal

Your child is a special, one-of-a-kind human being the likes of which the world has never seen. And chances are they'll lead an ordinary life not that different from your own. Right now, there are literally billions of amazing, creative, and brilliant people who will never do anything particularly amazing, creative, or brilliant. Never believe anything you read in a letter of recommendation. Or an obituary.

That's okay. Your kid doesn't have to be a once-in-a-generation talent to lead a good life. Being a genius at something doesn't come with a high job-satisfaction rate. Tortured artists seldom die of old age surrounded by loved ones. It's almost impossible in a world of drugs, guns, and sandwiches on toilets.

That's not a message overachieving parents want to hear. They expect their kid to set the world on fire and earn the

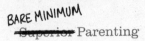
rewards that come with it: wealth, prestige, and—if there's time—happiness. But your child will turn out better if you don't try for any of those goals—not even the last one. The best things in life happen by accident.

To succeed as a parent—and outperform most overachieving parents in the process—you simply need to raise a kid who hits these three benchmarks:

1. They can support themselves.
2. They aren't a social deviant.
3. They don't blame you for everything that's wrong with their life.

Your goal as a bare minimum parent is to achieve all three in the easiest way possible. The result will be a functional adult you can be proud of, or at least one you can make move out of your house. Don't be intimidated by overachieving parents who aim higher. The only thing they'll hit is their kid. When you shoot for the stars, the bullets fall back to earth.

Boiling down child-rearing to those terms makes raising a kid seem easy, and in the parenting world, easy means wrong. But not in my book. Here's a closer look at all three benchmarks to show you why successful parenting is so simple even I can do it. It's hard to set the bar any lower than that.

And Stay Out

The fastest way to tell if your child turned out okay is if you can get rid of them. Gently shoving a kid out the door is the crowning achievement of any parent's life. But your kid isn't going anywhere unless they have a job. That's why raising your child to support themselves is the first benchmark of successful parenting. Without gainful employment, your kid will live with you forever—unless you're okay with them being homeless. After the tenth time they put an empty milk jug back in the fridge, you just might be.

As a bare minimum parent, you mainly want your kid to pay their own bills and not hit you up for money every month. At some point, the freeloading has to stop. It's just a shame it doesn't end earlier. Good luck getting grocery money from a toddler.

When it comes to your child's future job, the money matters, because if they don't make any, that money will come from you. Interpretive pottery-making might be a fulfilling career, but unless your child can find someone to pay for existential angst as expressed through clay dishes, you'll have to support them financially until you die. Or until they die. Kilns are more dangerous than they look.

Never encourage your kid down a path that could lead to them living in your basement. You don't have to actively discourage them from choosing a fun but impoverishing career. Just sit back and watch as the invisible hand of the free market slaps them in the face. The best lessons are the ones that leave a mark.

The Price of Luxury

Successful children need enough money to make it on their own, but not much more than that. Contrary to what overachieving parents might tell you, your kid doesn't need to be a

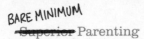
millionaire for you to be proud of them. Far from it. Rich people are some of the biggest failures I know. Well, that I know of. You've read enough of this book to guess I don't have any rich friends. Or any friends at all.

Once your child is no longer living paycheck to paycheck, wage increases don't make life much easier. Sure, extra money can speed up retirement or help put the next generation through college, but in terms of day-to-day living, there's only so much that money can do. The truth is the average person in Western civilization today is better off than the richest kings in Europe centuries ago. If you want pepper, you get it by going to the grocery store, not by sending a fleet of galleons around the world. Although you'll still complain if you forgot your coupon.

The biggest benefit of wealth is not what it lets people do, but what it lets them get out of doing. The upper class can pay someone to do all their grunt work for them. Unpleasant tasks like cooking, cleaning, and child-rearing can be foisted upon the hired help. Anything worth doing is worth paying someone else to do for minimum wage or less.

But rich people who rise above life's trivial hassles find a new level of even more trivial hassles to complain about. We all do it to some degree. History is just a sliding scale of grievances where people get equally angry over increasingly minor setbacks. Someone who lost their entire family to the plague in the 1300s complained just as much as someone today who suffers from slow Wi-Fi. Don't count on them to gain perspective, either. It would take too long to Google it.

Rich people's complaints are on the same sliding scale of grievances as everybody else. They're just further along, which puts them at grave risk from the rest of us. It's hard to hear a CEO complain about their heated toilet seat being too warm without wanting to punch someone in the face. Revolutions have started for less.

If your kid grows up to have a fridge full of food, a liquor cabinet full of booze, and a TV full of channels, there's not much more they need. There's no reason to push them to be rich. In fact, keeping your kid middle class could save their life. No one wants to be caught on the wrong side of the toilet seat rebellions.

One of Us

Life is not a popularity contest. With that being said, if everybody hates your kid, you lose. There are times when it pays not to be the least-liked person in a group. Elections come to mind. So do overladen boats where you have to decide who to throw overboard.

That's why, as a parent, you must stop your kid from being a social deviant. Your child doesn't have to be the most beloved person in the neighborhood. Just keep them from being singled out as an enemy of the state. Obvious marks of failure include exile, jail sentences, and viral articles that make everyone despise your kid. Next time, don't let your child write a post titled "Why I Hate Kittens." Or at least disown them first.

This is another benchmark where overachieving parents fall short. They want their kid to be loved by all, not from a desire to spread peace and harmony, but because of their own egos. If an overachieving parent is the best, then their child must also be the best. And if you refuse to acknowledge their kid's greatness, well, just be glad pistol duels are illegal everywhere but Texas and Vermont.

It's unrealistic to expect everyone to love your child, regardless of your kid's merits. People hate each other for good reasons and bad reasons and no reason at all. At best, we grudgingly tolerate other humans—and the annoyances that come with them—to stop civilization from collapsing. If people expressed how they really felt when they heard someone chewing cereal, every family breakfast would turn into *The Purge*. Keep those napkins handy.

You'll never truly know how much other people like your kid, but chances are it's less than you think. That's fine. Just make sure your child isn't so bad that people express their displeasure by forming an angry mob. If your kid's only exercise is running from torches and pitchforks, you've failed as a parent.

Beyond those basic criteria, the socialization goals for bare minimum parenting are pretty, well, minimal. A successful child can, when necessary, interact with other human beings without causing an incident. If your kid can go to the store without setting anything on fire, you've done a passable job of raising them. And if they can't resist burning stuff, there's always online shopping. Just block the sites that sell matches.

Different Kinds of Social Deviants You Might Raise

Deviant	Pro	Con
Burglar	They can support themselves.	They might get hired by a party of dwarves.
Ninja	They're quiet.	It's hard to enforce curfew.

Gang Leader	At least they showed some initiative.	They won't let you join.
Furry	Animal costumes will keep them warm.	It would've been easier to get a real dog.
Heavy Breather	They're well oxygenated.	They could become Dark Lord of the Sith.
Open-Mouth Chewer	They eat what you cooked.	They make you lose your lunch.
Late Library Book Returner	They're literate.	They're evil incarnate.

Not My Fault

The third benchmark is the one that will come up the most in your daily life. For you to be successful, your child must blame someone other than you for all their problems. I'd say they need to take personal responsibility, but that's not how people work. Even when we make mistakes, it's because someone else forced us into them. Nobody eats too much, drinks too much, or has too much sex through any fault of their own. Any excesses are a result of diseases or disorders brought on by bad genes or tragic life circumstances beyond our control. Except in the case of your child, it sort of is within your control. Because you're the person who created them, both their genes and their life circumstances are your fault. Way to ruin everything. You really are a parent.

This is yet another area where overachieving parents make a serious mistake. Rather than simply dodging the blame, overachieving parents try to solve the underlying problem. But if you try to fix something, you're basically admitting it was your fault in the first place. That's why the most adult thing to do as a parent when you notice a problem is to stick your hands in your pockets and nonchalantly walk away. Let some overachieving parent swoop in and take the fall instead. They can't help themselves.

You can't make someone love you. You can't even make them respect you. But as a bare minimum parent, you can trick them into not blaming you for everything. The world is falling apart, and the damage trickles down to the rest of us. Use that to your advantage. Make sure any problems you cause don't stand out above all the other issues plaguing society. You'll be fine as long as you aren't worse than global warming.

There's no shortage of alternative scapegoats. Blame Republicans. Blame Democrats. Blame any word ending in "ism." Blame corporations or protesters or college professors or rednecks. It doesn't matter where you place the blame as long as it isn't on you. The goal isn't to further a social cause. It's to stop your kid from slandering you behind your back for the rest of your life. When I say bare minimum, I mean it.

Forget to Smile

The most important benchmark is the one that's NOT on the list: happiness.

To overachieving parents, it seems like there's nothing wrong with keeping your child smiling. Happy kids whine less, throw fewer temper tantrums, and are less likely to write a tell-all memoir bashing your parenting. There are few things worse than having to read an entire book to find out why your kid hates you. That's what passive-aggressive text messages are for.

As a bare minimum parent, I'm not saying you should give your kid a wretched childhood. But making their happiness your top priority is the fastest way to ruin their life.

Think about it. My two-year-old is only happy when she's playing in toilet water. That doesn't make her successful, even though she's very good at it. There are no trophies for defiling a bathroom.

Happiness is an emotional pleasure response. When my toddler splashes toilet water everywhere, her brain is flooded with endorphins. But that doesn't mean it's good for her or anyone else. It certainly doesn't make me happy when I have to bleach the entire bathroom.

If happiness is your only goal for your kid, you might as well buy them heroin. There's no one more joyful than a drug addict in the middle of a high, even as it literally kills them. The lesson here is unmistakable: We don't know what's good for us, and too much happiness is fatal.

I don't want my two-year-old to grow up to be a hormone junkie or a serial toilet-water splasher. That's why I don't beat myself up when she's unhappy. As a bare minimum parent, I just want her to be self-sufficient, reasonably social, and reluctant to blame me for everything that's wrong with her life. If that fills her existence with gloom, so be it. At least she'll be a functional human being. Take that, everyone who's trying to get their kids on reality TV.

Activities That Make Kids Happy

Activity	Pro	Con
Taking a Toy from Another Kid	They gain a toy.	They gain an enemy.
Eating Candy	Buys you a few minutes of quiet.	Buys your kid's dentist a new car.
Popping Balloons	Makes a fun bang.	Enrages evil clowns.
Drawing on the Walls	Allows your kid to express themselves through art.	Makes you express yourself through profanity.
Digging Holes in the Backyard	You might find pirate treasure.	You'll definitely find ways to kill grass.
Knocking Over Someone Else's Block Building	Releases aggressive energy.	It's potential terrorist training.
Flushing Random Objects	Gets rid of excess toys.	Only until a plumber pulls them back out.
Rolling Around in Toxic Waste	Might make them superheroes.	Will certainly make a mess.

The Road to Success

Happy or not, your kid needs to hit all three benchmarks to become a functional adult. Keep these metrics in mind as you read the rest of this book. Write them down. Get them tattooed on your arm. Or maybe just buy a highlighter. I don't know, you do you.

Having a self-sufficient, nondeviant kid who doesn't blame you for everything isn't something new parents fantasize about. But after you've seen a few kids go wrong, you'll appreciate the beautiful simplicity of my approach. You're not raising the next Mozart or Einstein. But if you follow my method, you won't raise the next Charles Manson, either. If you're looking for a life goal, a good one is, "Don't raise a serial killer."

Instead, you'll rear an average person who means the world to you but seems more or less unremarkable to everyone else. That's what stressed-out, overachieving parents will end up with, too. They'll just waste more effort getting there. They're still trying to solve parenthood with an abacus while you're using a supercomputer. If you run into trouble, don't go back to the old ways. Just reboot and try again.

Luckily, you'll have plenty of chances for a fresh start. Biology provides a margin for error that overachieving parents fail to take advantage of. The bad news is you're about to make more mistakes than you can possibly imagine. The good news is nobody will remember them, not even your kid.

Chapter 3
You Make a Difference
Won't

Imagine this scene: A prestigious scientist stands up to receive a prestigious science award. After being handed the prize—something prestigious like a fifty-dollar gift certificate to the lab coat store—the scientist takes their spot behind the podium, well, prestigiously, because I don't own a thesaurus. The crowd falls silent in anticipation of whatever prestigious science words they're about to hear.

The winning scientist clears their throat.

"I'd like to thank my mother for breastfeeding me," they say. "Thank you, and good night."

Mic drop.

Cue the applause. The audience is on its feet. The geology section forms a mosh pit. A chemistry professor crowd-surfs. A lone biologist goes streaking.

Does something seem off about this scenario?

Not the partying, of course. Lab coats are made for hiding flasks.

The flaw is that no scientist at an awards ceremony has ever thanked their mom for breastfeeding them. Or for using formula. Or for doing pretty much anything before the scientist was old enough to remember it because, well, they don't remember it.

Countless factors played a role in putting that scientist on the podium, but none of them can be traced back to the ostensibly life-or-death decisions new parents beat themselves up over every day. No matter how badly you mess up, one wrong parenting decision won't turn a potential academic into a hobo who talks to cats. And even if it did, houses are overrated and everybody loves strays.

As a parent, you need to cut yourself some slack, especially for decisions when your child is very young. Almost any choice you make will probably be okay. There's no need to invent reasons to feel like a failure. There will be plenty of real reasons later on.

The Missing Link

When your kid looks back on their childhood, they won't care if you chose the right brand of stroller or co-slept or bought mentally stimulating toys marketed under the name of a famous theoretical physicist. Although, for the record, everything is stimulating to a baby. They're blown away by finding their own toes. And there are ten of those things, so that's a lot of excitement.

This isn't just a case of kids being ungrateful. There's legitimately no evidence the stuff early parenting books go on and on about makes any difference long term. A baby in the eighty-fifth growth percentile isn't any more likely to be the first person on Mars than a baby in the seventieth percentile. You're raising a child, not a pumpkin. There's no blue ribbon awarded by weight.

The connection between early parenting decisions and a child's success later in life is so tenuous that no one has even studied it—that I know of. Again, I did absolutely no research for this book. If there were such a study, I wouldn't read it anyway, so it might as well not exist. I take this bare minimum stuff seriously.

This lack of connection is obvious to anyone who takes a step back and looks at the big picture. That's why new parents never figure it out. They don't have time for perspective. They're too busy dodging baby pee.

Selective Enrollment

Nowhere is this lack of context clearer than in the struggle to find the right daycare. Landing a spot in one of the best child-care facilities is just as hard as getting into a top college—and nearly as expensive. But nobody stops to ask how attending a lesser daycare would impact their child's life. The answer, of course, is "not at all." No defendant has ever gotten off the hook by telling a judge, "It's not my fault, Your Honor. I went to a subpar preschool." That excuse might play well in the court of parental opinion, but it will still get your kid twenty-five to life.

Yet try telling that to any parent who spent six months shopping for a daycare before they were even pregnant. They probably still ended up on a two-year waiting list. It's never too early to find the right strangers to raise your child.

Again, not that it matters. Getting your kid into a top-tier daycare won't turn your child into a genius. Even the most academically aggressive teachers don't start SAT prep work while children are still in diapers. A kid can't comprehend the mysteries of the universe when they're still baffled by the toilet.

Important Lessons Kids Learn at Daycare

Lesson	Why It Matters
Don't bite.	Cannibalism is frowned upon in most societies.
Share.	The communists won after all.
Play nice with others.	It's best if your enemies don't know they're your enemies.
Eat fast.	An unfinished snack is a vulnerable snack.
Respect authority.	Preschool is a tough time to start an insurrection.
Glitter is amazing.	Bring it home on everything. Your parents won't mind.
Cows say moo.	Not sure why it matters. It's not like you can talk to them.

If daycare choices don't matter, why do parents stress out about them? Because life is a competition. If someone else gets their kid into a top daycare and you don't, you'll feel like a failure by comparison. For overachieving parents, the road to success starts the moment their baby leaves the birth canal. Careful. Those first few steps are slippery.

You might not think you're competitive, but wait until the first time an overachieving parent gets their kid in somewhere exclusive that you couldn't get yours. Expect some patronizing reassurance from your fellow mom or dad. Their lips will say, "Your daycare is fine," but their eyes will say, "It's basically a crack house." You won't remember much after that. You can piece it together the next morning in your holding cell.

The Unending War

The competition for the best daycare is a minor bush war compared with the full-scale conflict between working parents and stay-at-home parents. There are only two choices, which in the minds of many people means one option is right and one is wrong. The pressure couldn't be higher. There are no special coffee mugs for the world's second-best mom or dad. But at least there's beer, which is like an award you give yourself. Participation never tasted so sweet.

If you're a working parent, you'll sacrifice quality time with your child. If you're a stay-at-home parent, you'll sacrifice your career. There's no choice that won't leave you feeling conflicted. Certainty is for the childless.

There's no way to say anything on this topic without offending people on both sides of the issue, so I'll settle this in the least controversial way possible: Everybody is wrong. But you're only wrong because you think there's a right answer.

Kids too young for school are too young to remember if you worked or stayed home, and even when they're older, they won't ask about what you did in the past. They'll be more focused on themselves than they ever will be on you. Narcissism is the great equalizer.

Besides, many parents pick one option and then switch, staying home for part of their kid's childhood and working for part of it. Good luck remembering for yourself where the line was between the two. There's no chance your kid will stash that information in their memory banks. You'll be lucky if they remember you.

Choose whichever approach you want. Your decision has no bearing on whether your kid will become a prestigious scientist or a homeless cat whisperer. Although if they're really ambitious, they can do both. The Nobel Prize committee would love a purr-to-speech translator.

The people in your own life prove that sending your kid to daycare and staying home to watch them yourself both work. Think about everyone you've met as an adult. Without knowing anything about their childhoods, could you tell if their parents worked or stayed home? If you say yes, you're lying. Or psychic, in which case, why did you buy this book? You could have saved money and just read my mind.

That's not what overachieving parents want to hear, of course. And while they should relax because both choices are right, they're more likely to panic because both options feel wrong. As soon as you have a child, you gain the unique ability to feel terrible about yourself no matter what. Worst superpower ever.

The mere fact that you think you're a bad parent proves you're at least an okay one. Terrible parents don't spend their days twisted in knots with anxious introspection. Don't feel bad about feeling bad. It just shows you're not such a bad parent after all.

How Guilty Parents Feel Over Different Issues

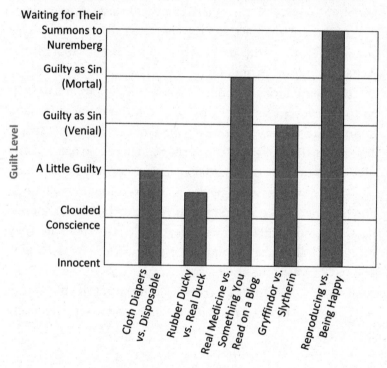

Without a Trace

Don't be discouraged by the futility of your choices. From a bare minimum standpoint, it's exactly what you want. And this isn't just good news for which daycare you choose or whether you work or stay at home. Almost nothing you do in your kid's early childhood can be proven decisively to either help or hurt them later in life. A parent's greatest tool isn't love; it's plausible deniability.

In later years, when your kid is old enough to remember and judge what you do, your actions will carry more weight. But until then, you have a blank check to raise them however you want. Don't let this power go to your head. It's more fun if you keep your brain out of it.

The possibilities are endless. Make your kid wear a dragon costume every day till they're four. Tell them the automatic doors at the grocery store won't open unless they breakdance. Teach them that cows are called sharks. There's no harm in any of it—until one day they hear the *Jaws* music and start to moo.

Kids have survived questionable parenting for millennia, and our species is no worse for it. Young children can bounce back from anything because they won't remember it. They evolved this amnesia as much for your benefit as for theirs. You have a solid four or five years to mess up without any consequences. Parenting is mostly trial and error. Get your errors out of the way early on and no one will be the wiser—especially not you.

Pick Your Poison

Your child's forgetfulness will help you hit all three parenting benchmarks without really working at it. Your child is more likely to get a job if they don't remember how you agonized over whether to stay in the workforce or stay home with them.

Your early decisions won't turn your child into a social deviant because your kid won't remember they ever happened. But if your child does somehow turn out wrong, they can't blame you because that same amnesia means early on you were parenting in stealth mode. Honestly, you might be better off if you forget that part of their life, too. You can't feel guilty about what you don't remember. What were we talking about again?

The truth is it's almost impossible to ruin your child with basic parenting decisions you make in the first years of their life. Your mistakes won't hurt anyone as long as you don't freak out about them. Stress isn't great for your long-term health. Panicking is fine if you need a quick burst of adrenaline for something practical, like lifting a tractor off a baby or fighting off a zombie swarm. But otherwise it strains your heart and makes it that much more likely you'll die early. At least that will make your parenting choices simpler.

While most of the time your child will turn out about the same no matter what you do, I can say decisively that your kid will be better off if you live than if you die. Growing up an orphan almost always works against children. For every Harry Potter, there's a Tom Riddle. The world doesn't need more Horcruxes.

So take a deep breath and stay alive. It doesn't matter which decisions you make as long as you're still around to make them. You're doing okay at parenting just by having a pulse.

Chapter 4

~~It Takes a Village~~

Fending Off the Mob

In the long run, all of your early parenting decisions will work out just fine. Unfortunately, in the short term, you leave yourself open to criticism.

Consider every parent's worst nightmare:

You're at a park with your kid. They're hungry, as they always are when you're away from food. If you had a three-course meal laid out in front of them, they wouldn't take a bite, but the second you're out in public, they're starving. They don't need food to fill them up. They feed on your frustration.

But you're not interested in child physiology. You just want the whining to stop before your head explodes. The final countdown has begun.

With seconds to spare, you spot salvation: a vending machine. It glimmers in the distance like an oasis in the desert. You grab your ungrateful child by the hand and half-drag them to the promised land. But up close, deliverance doesn't look so appetizing. None of the packages in the vending machine have the words modern parents crave, like "organic," "soy," or "gluten-free." Instead, this metal and glass box of broken dreams is full of calorie-dense, chocolate-covered foodstuffs with no nutritional value whatsoever. Sure, you grew up on these snacks, but that parenting group you're in told you this stuff is basically poison. Then again, your kid's whining has gone up thirty decibels and your brain is throbbing like you should call the bomb squad. Buy the damn candy.

You move to pay the machine. But with your hand an inch from the coin slot, you freeze. You have a bad feeling about this. You glance to the left. You glance to the right. The coast is clear. There isn't another human being within two miles. No one will ever know the desperate, unforgivable thing you did today.

You buy the candy bar and hand it to your child. It's gone in a flash. They didn't even chew. And just like that, the whining stops. For the first and only time since you became a parent, you relax.

You fool! Suddenly, a voice pierces the quiet. "You let your kid eat that?!" You look up. It's another parent. Where did they come from? Were they hiding behind the vending machine? That's not weird at all.

The other parent looks at your happy child and then back at you. All you did was give your kid a candy bar, but you might as well have hit them with a lead pipe. You know what's coming, but you're powerless to stop it. Your arms and legs don't work. You're paralyzed by guilt.

The other parent aims a judgmental finger directly at your chest.

"You."

Time stops. Your kid stands still for the first time ever.

"Are."

Your life flashes before your eyes. Did you really dress like that? No wonder your life turned out so badly.

"A."

Your heart thuds so hard it cracks two ribs. Does your insurance cover self-inflicted injuries from bad parenting? Trick question. No doctor would touch you now.

"Bad."

The B word. Not the B word.

"Parent."

At least they kept it gender neutral. Very progressive of them.

For a second, you stand there like a movie samurai who's been stabbed so cleanly they didn't even feel it. Then the world spins. You fall.

The park explodes with motion. Police in military gear storm out of the shadows and drag your kid off to an orphanage—the really bad kind with mean nuns and gruel. Who cares if your child has another parent? They can't be trusted. They loved someone as awful as you.

Your child screams in terror.

"Why did you give me that candy bar?! You knew this would happen! You knew!"

As your vision fades, you smell smoke. Somewhere in the distance, your parents burn your old photos. Soldiers topple your statue in a crowded square. Your old classmates unfriend you.

Then, mercifully, you die.

This is truly the worst day in the history of the world—except for the part where none of that fallout happened.

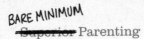
To the shock of everyone—including you—you didn't die when a stranger criticized your parenting. The SWAT team didn't take your kid. Your mom and dad didn't stop loving you. Your statue didn't get toppled, mostly because there wasn't one. Your former classmates remain indifferent to your existence.

You probably didn't even fall over, though if you did, there's no shame in it. Gravity is a wily foe.

It turns out being criticized by someone you don't know has no bearing on you whatsoever. That doesn't stop non-bare minimum parents from letting it ruin their lives.

How Normal, Well-Adjusted Parents React to Criticism

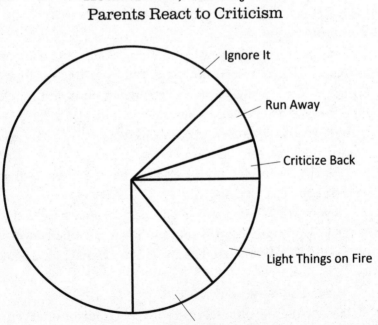

To an outside observer, that scene in the park played out very differently. You bought your kid a candy bar. Another parent was a jerk about it. Then everyone went their separate ways. That's it. End of consequences.

A stranger can't stop you from feeding your kid a candy bar. There's no challenge flag or booth review. It's not up for a vote, and, unless the candy bar is linked to terrorism, the government won't intervene. In this one area, you have absolute, unchecked authority. Abuse it at will.

The only thing a third party can do about your parenting is say something that makes you mad. That's the full extent of their powers. If you brood all night about what they said, they win. But if you shrug it off, they're powerless against you. Your bully will have no choice but to take a hard look at their life and reform their ways. Just kidding. They'll go harass someone else.

High School Never Ends

As a bare minimum parent, you shouldn't care what anyone else thinks, including me. Responding to criticism, constructive or otherwise, is too much work. Apathy doesn't just make life easier; it makes you unstoppable. You're Superman, but without the Kryptonite—or the desire to help your fellow man.

Unfortunately, few parents lazy their way to enlightenment. Instead of letting hurtful words drift by with Zen-like serenity, parents get in six-hour flame wars about the best method for potty training or what to put on toast. At least I do. I refuse to concede the last word to Mr. I-Only-Use-Goat-Butter.

If other people's opinions can't stop you, why do you care if other parents judge you? Two words: peer pressure. You want to fit in and be liked by everyone, especially the people who hate you. Sure, you tell yourself you don't care what other people think, but then you're devastated when you post something about parenting that doesn't get any likes. And heaven forbid someone in the comment section disagrees with you. It could ruin your day or even your life. At the very least, it will ruin your friendship. Social media started as a way for people to talk to each other, but more often it's the reason people never speak to each other again.

The Most Valid Reasons to End a Friendship

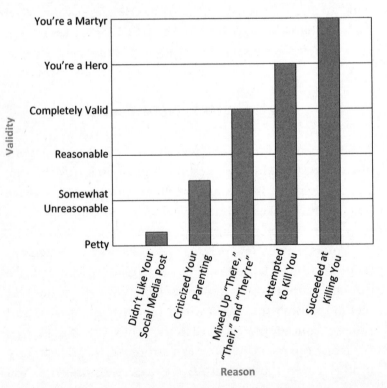

If this self-destructive cycle sounds uncomfortably familiar, that's because it is—it's just like high school. When you look back at those four years, it's hard to remember why you tried to impress people you would never see again. Instead of enjoying yourself during a stage of life that had few lasting consequences, you obsessed over minor things like dances, gossip, or what to put on toast. Again, maybe that last one was just me. At the time, it seemed like those were the only things that mattered, but they stopped mattering forever thirty seconds after you graduated. You spent four years stressing out for nothing. At least you would never make that mistake again.

Enter parenthood. You're stressed beyond belief about minor decisions that have no long-term impact on your child's life. In that desperate hour, you turn to other people for advice. Big mistake. You don't want people to tell you what to do. You just want everyone to tell you that what you're already doing is right. You're a perfect parent just the way you are.

But the world doesn't work that way, especially in the Internet Age. Anonymity lets people take extreme positions without reprisal. Tact comes not from a desire for civility, but from the fear of being punched in the face. Remove that and random strangers aren't afraid to tell you that using the wrong type of bottle nipple makes you worse than Hitler. Would those people ever say that to you in person? Absolutely not. And for the record, Hitler's bottle nipple stance remains unclear.

Instead of being embraced by the masses, you feel bad about your parenting decisions because other people told you to. You want to switch to the popular side, but you can't because it doesn't exist. There's no consensus. The only thing anyone can agree on is that everyone else is wrong.

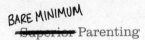
For a bare minimum parent, the best solution is also the easiest: Ignore it all. There's no such thing as winning an argument on the internet, a place where no one has changed their mind since 1998. Don't ask for advice, and don't give it. Unless you're writing a bare minimum parenting book in a shameless cash grab. Then use your best judgment.

The only time it's okay to ask a question on the internet is if you don't care about the answer. If you're open to buying either of two brands of diapers, ask for advice. But if you already bought a year's supply of one or the other, don't bother. You'll just end up infuriated when someone says you made the wrong choice and doomed your kid to twelve months of inferior poop containment. No matter how messy it gets, it's still easier to change a diaper than a mind.

Issues People Never Change Their Mind On

Issue	Reason
Literally Anything	You're right and everyone else is wrong. Duh.

Judging If You're Being Judged

Parent shaming is easy to detect on the internet because it's all there in black and white—or purple or blue, depending on the font colors. The happier the typography, the more brutal the insult. My face does NOT look like a stupid hamster butt, SallyRulz13. People on the internet don't hesitate to call you every name in the book. I'm not sure what book, but it must be a short one. Most of its words only have four letters.

Parents in the real world don't use those words to your face. They watch what they say because a child never forgets a swear word. That's what makes it so hard to tell if other parents are judging you. Most of the time, they won't say it out loud. Parents can convey an incredible amount of information with just their eyes. A single look can say anything from "Stop that!" to "What did I do to be cursed with this child?" If you're wondering, it was sex.

There's a fine line between being wary of silent judgment and being paranoid. You're not the center of the universe. Not every parent who looks in your direction is judging you. Like you, they have a million other things on their mind. In fact, they're probably only looking over at you to make sure you're not judging them. Now you have another reason to feel bad.

When you suspect other people are judging you when they're really not, what you're actually doing is judging yourself. You assume whatever you're doing is worthy of condemnation. Maybe it is. Only you know if letting your kid eat chocolate chips with maple syrup counts as a balanced breakfast. If you were confident in your choices, you wouldn't be afraid of what other parents think. Instead, you'd parent as publicly as possible to receive the accolades you deserve. Changing a diaper deserves a pat on the back; getting your kid to behave in the grocery store warrants a standing ovation; and defusing a temper tantrum in a crowded restaurant deserves a ticker-tape parade. Just remember, that key to the city isn't a real key. If you want to break into people's houses, you'll have to do it the old-fashioned way.

Loud and Proud

On those rare occasions when another parent berates you face-to-face, take it as a compliment. They're accusing you of parenting differently than they are. Perfect. They don't know the right way to raise a child. They don't even know the right way to be an adult.

People don't criticize complete strangers out of the goodness of their hearts. They do it because your choices make them feel insecure about their own. Either that or you're so terrible that other people can't avoid speaking up. If you let your kids juggle knives or do unlicensed electrical work, maybe they have a point. But let's assume whatever you're doing won't lead to serious bodily harm. I'm teaching you to be a lazy parent, not a deadly one.

As long as parents raise their kids in contrasting ways, they'll lash out to prove their method is the right one. That's why campaigns to end shaming are so misguided. If centuries of armed conflict have proven anything, it's that human beings aren't great at tolerating minor differences. Just be glad your argument over baby formula ended with parent shaming and not the Thirty Years' War.

Top Parent-Shaming Topics

Topic	Why It Matters
Breastfeeding vs. Bottle Feeding	If your baby doesn't gain enough weight, they might lose at baby sumo.

Co-sleeping	No idea. I slept through it.
Traditional Name vs. Something Unique	It's up to you if you ever want anyone to spell your kid's name right.
Sugar vs. Sugar-Free	You may or may not be raising an ant.
Bedtimes	If your kid doesn't get enough sleep at night, they might get tired and nap during the day. The horror.
Potty-Training Age	No one wants a thirty-year-old in diapers.
Letting Your Kid Watch R-Rated Movies	Your child might learn something scary about the world, like that it sucks.
Helping Your Kid with Their Homework	Should your kid fail on their own or fail with your help?

The Struggle Is Real

Peer pressure from other parents isn't easy to resist. That's why it's called "peer pressure," not "peer opinions you don't care about." But what makes these people your peers? All you have in common is that you have a kid. That doesn't make you part of an exclusive club. Creating a human being isn't unique or special. It's so easy, people literally do it by accident.

Stop pretending other people's opinions matter just because they're parents, too. It's easy enough to ignore others' opinions in nonparenting areas. You don't get sucked into a spiral of self-doubt when someone tells you how to vote. In

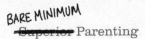
fact, you cling to your own position even harder. A fellow parent's opinions on bedtimes or homework or curfew are no more relevant to your life than their opinion on who should be president. Shrug them off accordingly. Or use a campaign yard sign to smack them.

Once your kid is grown, you'll have nothing in common with these people. Get ahead of the curve and stop valuing their opinions now. This is the one time in bare minimum parenting when it's okay to work ahead. It's never too early to care less.

Avoidance Therapy

The easiest way to resist other people's opinions is to never hear them in the first place. You tell your kid to avoid circumstances where they'll face peer pressure. Take your own advice. Stay away from situations where people will judge you for parenting differently than the herd. It doesn't matter if they talk about you when you're not there. As the saying goes, absence makes your sanity grow stronger.

Avoiding parental peer pressure situations is even more important on the internet. There's no law that says you have to be on ten parenting forums at once. If you're shooting for the bare minimum, you should be in zero. Nobody needs that much advice. The human race managed to raise its kids just fine before comment sections and message boards. No one ever died because they didn't get enough likes.

Whether you achieve it by avoiding people or just by ignoring them, a firm indifference to other people's opinions will help you hit successful parenting benchmarks. Your child is less likely to be a social deviant if they follow your example and avoid all the stupid, dangerous things their friends try to pressure them into. And if your kid does blame you for their problems, you won't care as much because you can ignore them, too.

Just be prepared to need those opinion-blocking skills a lot. Other parents will criticize you for every decision you make—especially the ones you can't change, like when you decided to start a family. You don't have a time machine for a do-over. But if you did, you should forget about parent shaming and kill Hitler. Or at least find out his stance on bottle nipples.

Chapter 5
The ~~Right~~ Wrong Time to Have a Kid

When is the best time for a hurricane? Or an earthquake? How about a sandstorm? Have you ever said to yourself, "This is a good point in my life for a flood" or "I'm finally ready for that forest fire"?

No?

Then why do overachieving parents think there's a "right" time to have a kid? Children are a natural disaster every bit as devastating as an avalanche or a landslide. And they don't even require mountains of mud or snow to destroy your house. All they need is one permanent marker.

But overachieving parents think they have it all figured out. They plan to wait the perfect amount of time before they add their perfect child to their perfect life. Those parents are soon perfectly disappointed, and that's perfectly fine with me.

Bare minimum parents know that no matter how prepared you think you are for a kid, you'll never be fully ready. No amount of emotional, intellectual, or financial groundwork will ever make it easy to scrub poop off the wall. And, no, college parties won't train you in advance. You can't let your kid sleep it off on the cold bathroom floor, no matter how much they deserve it.

However, while there's no ideal time to reproduce, different times are challenging for different reasons. This chapter will examine the benefits and drawbacks of having a kid at different ages for both bare minimum and overachieving parenting. But don't skip this section if you already have a kid. The best mistakes are worth repeating.

Likelihood of Getting Pregnant

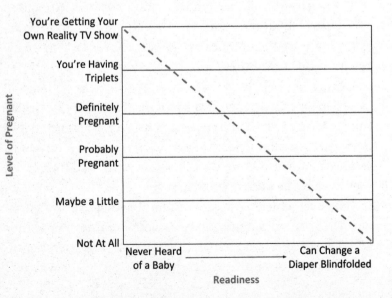

High Fertility, Low Intelligence: The Teenage Years

Nothing good ever happens in high school. This includes conceiving a child. If you have a baby before you can legally vote, there's a 99 percent chance it was a mistake. That leaves a 1 percent chance you did it on purpose. May God have mercy on your soul.

Being children themselves, teens are unprepared to raise a kid, so they're bare minimum parents by default. In fact, teens are so bad at parenting, it sometimes makes parenting easier. If you procreate in your teenage years and you still live at home, there's a chance your parents will raise the kid for you. They won't be happy about it, but if they ever watched you care for a pet, they'll be reluctant to let you care for a child. To this day, no one knows how your goldfish ran away.

From an ethical standpoint, there's nothing worse than pawning off your child on your own parents. But from a bare minimum perspective, it's a job well done. This is a book about how to be a lazy parent, not a good person. Morals are too much work.

Ultimately, however, the convenience of dumping your kid on someone else isn't worth it. The guilt trips could be fatal. Your parents will blame you for everything wrong in your kid's life, and your kid will blame you, too. Every good sob story starts with, "My parents were just teenagers when they had me." The third benchmark of successful parenting is to avoid blame, not to absorb as much of it as humanly possible. There's no time limit on voicing that particular grievance, either. When you're ninety-six and your kid is eighty, they'll still say they could've been president if only they'd had more mature parents early on. Maybe it's for the best they didn't succeed. The only thing worse than a bratty child is a bratty child with nuclear launch codes.

Teenage pregnancy is an easy trap to fall into. Your teen years are when you're the least ready to become a parent mentally and emotionally, but the most ready to become a parent physically. Your body is primed to pump out kids at an early age because it's calibrated for the life spans of the last Ice Age. Watch out for stampeding mammoths. But this conflicts with society, which says you don't have to be an adult until you're well past college. Your reproductive system and your maturity level are moving at two different speeds. In the race between your brain and your libido, the loser is human civilization.

At least if you do accidentally become a teen parent, you can't overachieve at anything. You'll be lucky to finish high school. Your kid won't take second place to a secondary education, no matter how much it would help your future. Babies are bad at seeing the big picture. And without that diploma, you won't have many job options. The few there are will soon be done by robots. Consider becoming one yourself. No one messes with the cyborg at the drive-thru.

As a young bare minimum parent, you'll have a few advantages over older parents, trivial though they may seem. For starters, you'll be too young and dumb to realize you're screwed. Older parents have the wisdom and maturity to recognize approaching disasters. They can't stop them; they just look on helplessly as misfortune approaches from a distance. But if you're a teen parent, you'll be blissfully unaware of the challenges ahead. You'll be worry-free until life sucker-punches you in the face. Always wear a mouthguard.

Pros and Cons of Being a Teen Parent

Pro	Con
You'll be fast enough to chase down your child.	You'll have to deal with your kid that much sooner.
It's not your fault if you don't know any better.	That won't help your child's odds of survival.
You won't get tired.	You'll have more waking hours to make life-ruining mistakes.
You'll bounce back from any parenting-related injuries.	You'll be ready to hurt yourself again sooner.
Other people will pay for stuff since you'll have no income.	You'll owe everyone favors for the rest of your life.
You'll beat your peers to all parenting milestones.	No one was racing you.

You'll also have more energy than at any other stage in your life. Sleepless nights with a newborn won't faze you since you would've been up that late anyway doing whatever pointless, time-wasting activities teens are into these days. I have no idea because I'm in bed by nine. You'll even have the energy to chase around a toddler, which you wouldn't if you had a kid later in life. This won't make your kid behave better, but you'll be able to catch disasters faster. With luck, you'll find that Lego pie before your kid turns on the microwave. It tastes better cold anyway.

Finally, if you have a kid when you're young, you'll have them around for more of your life. You'll spend the same eighteen years raising them, but you'll get more time with them when they're an adult than if you'd had them at a later age. They're less work at that stage, so it makes sense to maximize the easy years you live to see. That's more time with your best friend—or worst enemy. You won't know until it's too late. There are no returns for adult children.

Overachieving parents would never, ever consider becoming a parent during their teenage years. Bare minimum parents shouldn't, either. But if you somehow find yourself with a kid, embrace the few bare minimum advantages teen parents have and hope for the best. With a little luck, you'll survive your teenage years. With a lot of luck, your kid will, too.

A Degree and a Baby

Overachieving parents want to be "established" before they have a kid. In their fantasy world, that involves a committed relationship, a six-figure salary, and a celebrity photographer to capture their casual moments in six-hour-long photo shoots. There's nothing more candid than posing in designer clothes at a park you only visit once a year when you need family photos.

That's why the years immediately following college are still the exclusive territory of bare minimum parents. If you start a family in your early twenties, you have to be willing to do less with less. A twenty-two-year-old graduate is even poorer than a teen parent. A sixteen-year-old mom or dad is simply broke. But if you're a recent college graduate, you're in the hole. And you'll likely stay that way till you're buried in an actual hole. Your tombstone will say, "They ALMOST paid off their student

Pros and Cons of Raising a Kid in Your Early Twenties

Pro	Con
Your degree will show you know everything.	You won't.
You'll be a real adult.	Your age will confirm it. Your maturity level won't.
Staying up late will still be relatively easy.	You'll regret that lost sleep when you're older.
You'll save money.	By never having fun.
People won't give you strange looks for having a kid too young.	Just kidding. Judgment has no age limit.
You'll be old enough to buy alcohol.	No downside. This will save your life.

loans." Then the student loan company will repossess your coffin.

Also, most teen parents are expected to mooch off their parents. As a recent college graduate, you won't benefit from those lower standards. People will mistake you for an adult because you'll kind of look like one. You'll be expected to financially support your offspring, outrageous though that may sound. Becoming a grown-up is the second-most expensive mistake you'll ever make. The first is having a kid.

To add insult to injury, you'll be making the least money of your career. No matter what field you go into, you'll start at the bottom. You'll work longer and harder and for less money than your coworkers who have been there more years than

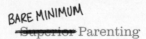
you. But if you stick with it and sacrifice decades of your life to the company, you'll get promoted high enough to exploit the people below you. The system works, unless you never move up and just get walked all over for your entire career, which is what happens to most of us.

Overachieving parents could never cope with those challenges, but as a bare minimum parent, you'll never be more ready than you are right then. College teaches you to get by with no money and even less sleep, so raising a kid will just be more of the same. The only difference is the struggle lasts eighteen years instead of four, and if you fail, your kid will be a social deviant who can't support themselves and blames you for all their problems. No pressure.

Middling Mid-to-Late Twenties

By their mid-to-late twenties, potential overachieving parents are done biding their time. They've moved up a few rungs on the corporate ladder by stepping on the faces of the people below them. Scuffed up their shoes, too. But now they have money, and that solves all problems. This is the best time to have a kid, right?

Wrong. This is just one of the many myths overachieving parents want you to believe, like that hard work is rewarded or that poverty is contagious. Stay quarantined on your own side of the tracks. Overachieving parents think that by waiting, they'll give their kid a more privileged life, but in reality, they become just as broke as everybody else by wasting their money on pointless upgrades. Instead of buying a basic crib, they will buy a super-deluxe model that costs four times as

Pros and Cons of Raising a Child in Your Mid-to-Late Twenties

Pro	Con
You'll have money.	Actually, if you're an overachieving parent, the store will have your money. You'll have a bunch of overpriced baby junk.
You'll understand life in all its wonder.	You'll understand life in all its horror.
You'll have a career.	You'll wreck your career.
You'll feel ready for a kid.	You'll walk right into a trap.
You'll be the median age of most first-time parents.	You'll have found yet another way to be completely average.
You'll have life experience.	That experience will tell you to run away.

much but still serves the same function of housing their kid in a nocturnal baby cage. But buying their child anything less than the best would make them a horrible mom or dad. They always give in to their guilt. The economy depends on it.

This is one of the worst stages in life to try to overdo it. If you're an overachieving parent in your mid-to-late twenties, not only will you waste all your extra money on those pointless upgrades, but you'll also have less energy to chase your kid. Eventually, you'll just lie down in the middle of the floor while your child rampages around you. Accept it. This is their house now.

You can still be a bare minimum parent at this stage, but it'll take more effort to do less work. You'll be tempted to use your increasing resources to try to make your child's life better. Resist. Spending more money on your kid won't turn them into a more functional adult, but it will turn you into a poorer one. You have my permission to be cheap, guilt-free. This book just paid for itself.

Thirsty Thirties

If you make it to your thirties before having a kid, you most likely have an incredible life. You travel, excel professionally, and have an extensive network of cherished friends. If you're an overachiever, it's the best time of your life. Too bad it's over.

There's no law that says you have to give up everything that makes life worth living when you have a kid, but for overachieving parents, it happens anyway. If you lived for work, you'll have to cut back. You can't put in eighty hours a week at the office and eighty hours at home with your kid. Well, technically you could, since there are 168 hours in a week. That leaves eight hours a week for sleep, which is a normal amount for a new parent.

Or maybe your pre-kid focus was on overachieving at your social life. Perhaps you met your regular crew every night at a bar where everybody knows your name. The best friends are the ones who enable your functional alcoholism. After kids, you'll lose touch with those people, both because you'll develop different interests and because friends are work. Even if they're willing to come over to your place, you'll just silently count down the minutes till they leave so you can go to

Pros and Cons of Raising a Child in Your Thirties

Pro	Con
Other people will think you had a kid at the perfect age.	You'll know that's a lie.
You likely did this on purpose.	What were you thinking?
You'll have even more life experience.	You'll miss experiencing life.
People will get off your back about when you're going to have a kid.	They'll get on your back about when you're going to have another.
You won't get carded at the liquor store anymore.	People will see how desperately you need a drink.

bed. Not that you'll stay asleep if you have a baby. The key to a full night's rest is starting your insomnia early.

Most overachievers wait until their thirties because, no matter what they were passionate about, they thought a kid would ruin it. And they were right. That's why people who put in the bare minimum at everything have the right idea. By not being passionate about work or a social life, they won't have anything to painfully give up, not even in their thirties. Kids can't ruin your life if you never had one in the first place.

Frantic Forties

Starting a family in your forties isn't usually on the radar for either overachieving or bare minimum parents, but there are plenty of reasons why it might happen anyway. Maybe you didn't find your partner until later in life. Or perhaps you had a partner, but the baby-making process didn't go as smoothly as you'd like. It's tough to know which parts go where, even with the instruction manual.

Whatever the reason, this isn't a position most parents end up in by choice. Even the procrastinators usually have their first kid in their late thirties. But the deadline for kids isn't as hard and fast as you might think, especially for people old enough to think they don't need to think about preventing kids at all. That's when they sneak up on you. Past a certain age, all surprises are bad surprises. Defend yourself accordingly.

If you have your first kid in your forties, you'll feel more pressure than ever to overachieve. Tragically, you won't be able to use poverty or youth as an excuse to cut corners. You'll have more financial stability and life experience than at any other stage. You'll be the adultest of adults. That might sound like a blessing and a curse, but it's actually just a double curse. Those aren't covered by your health insurance.

This is when the exhaustion that's been creeping into your life for the last two decades will finally reach its full potential. Add kids, and the only time you won't be eager for a nap is when you're already taking a nap, and even then you might dream about napping. The parent version of *Inception* would just be a tired mom slipping into a double coma.

Your body will give up, but your pride won't. Rather than doing the bare minimum on your own, you'll be tempted to

Pros and Cons of Raising a Child in Your Forties

Pro	Con
Your life is stable.	Your life WAS stable. Now you have a kid.
When you go to school functions, you'll be the experienced parent.	That's just a nice way of saying "old as hell."
You won't have trouble falling asleep at night.	You might not wake up.
You'll get to vicariously feel the joy of youth.	You'll feel older than ever.
Your midlife crisis will make you ready for a change.	Kids are a whole-life crisis.
You'll be old enough to tell "back in my day" stories.	Only use them if you want your kid to run away.

use your midlife money to hire a nanny to overachieve on your behalf. What could go wrong? Every kid needs a parental figure who can be fired at will.

In a shocking turn of events everyone saw coming, throwing money at your problem will only backfire. Normally, even when your kid blames you for everything, they still love you, which will almost make up for how difficult they make even the simplest things in your life. But if you pay someone else to parent for you, you'll still get all your kid's blame but none of their love, which will go to the nanny or robot butler depending on how far into the future you wait to reproduce. As for self-sufficiency, if you can't take care of your kid, how do you expect your kid to take care of themselves? They'll try to solve all their problems by outsourcing them to the lowest bidder. While that might be an admirably lazy approach, it's not a sustainable one. Eventually, they'll end up broke and bitter, just like you. They'll experience all the shame and disappointment of being a parent without ever having a kid. Maybe they're on to something.

In your forties, it's critical that you find just enough energy to be lazy. Don't overachieve, and don't pay anyone else to overachieve on your behalf. Parent with whatever you have left in the tank and you'll achieve the bare minimum for your kids. The easy way is always the best.

Too Old for This Stuff

If you're in your fifties or up and you're raising a kid, chances are they're not your own. If they are, congratulations. You're living proof that science can pull off almost any crime against nature. But in the more likely scenario, you're looking after someone else's offspring. Somewhere along the line, a biological parent dropped the ball and possibly the child, too. Luckily, both bounce.

It's doubtful this is your first time as a parent, but it's probably a surprise nonetheless. The child-rearing phase of your life is like chicken pox: Once you're over it, you're not supposed to get it again. But if you do, it's a whole lot worse.

By the time you're a retiree, you'll be well past your earnings prime. A lifetime of bad choices likely will have left you with a fixed income and little else. If you're forced to raise a kid on that, you might as well take your money and light it on fire. At least that will help with the heating bill.

Pros and Cons of Raising a Child When You're Old as Hell

Pro	Con
No idea.	Cons don't matter. You'll be dead soon anyway.

At that point, you'll be as poor as a teenager but with the exhaustion of the elderly. Overachieving is out of the question, but the bare minimum approach can once again save the day. No one will expect anything from you. As the guardian of last resort, you'll be the greatest adult in that child's life merely by keeping them alive. People will expect nothing from you, and that's all you'll have to give. You just might make it.

But you probably won't. That's good news, too. You'll be six feet underground before the kid is old enough to hate you. When you go, they'll still be in the age group where they think you're amazing. Plus you'll hit the third benchmark of successful parenting by default: No matter how badly they turn out, they'll never blame you for anything. You'll forever be the heroic grandparent who helped raise them, which is nice, even if it won't make you any less dead. Expect a nicely worded thank-you card on your tombstone.

Timing Is Everything

In short, being too young or too old is no excuse to try hard when you're raising a kid. It's easy to be a bare minimum parent in your teenage years, right after college, and from your forties on up. As for your mid-to-late twenties and thirties,

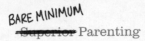

you'll feel immense pressure to overachieve. Don't give in. Laziness isn't a vice; it's a vocation. Answer the call—but not too fast. You don't want to seem too motivated.

Now that you know when to start having kids, the next question is, "When should you stop?" I have four children, but many people call it quits after one. Do they know something I don't? About child-rearing, that is. I've already proven my lack of knowledge on everything else.

Deciding how big a family to have is a deeply personal question with an individual answer specific to your life. No one can tell you how many kids are right for you. But nuance and tact are for better books. I have a one-size-fits-all answer for everybody. Time for me to plan your entire family.

Chapter 6

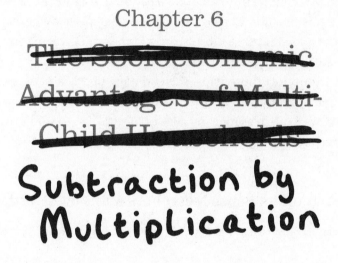

~~The Socioeconomic Advantages of Multi-Child Households~~

Subtraction by Multiplication

Imagine a startup car company invents an engine that runs on a special fuel. It could be anything, but since I'm hungry, let's say it's cereal. That would be revolutionary. Current fuel tanks don't do well if you add Lucky Charms.

Since there are no other cars on the market powered by sugary breakfast foods, this company—which I'll call Tasty Fuel-Os since it's my imaginary company and I can do whatever I want—starts from scratch.

First, Tasty Fuel-Os does extensive research and development to answer key questions. Can the same engine handle hearts, stars, horseshoes, clovers, AND blue moons? Does horsepower suffer if there's a prize in the box? Do pistons run better before or after you add the milk? Tasty Fuel-Os's scientists resolve these queries through experiments that are as painstaking as they are magically delicious.

After that, Tasty Fuel-Os erects a special one-of-a-kind factory. No other facility can build a car like this, mostly because it's a terrible idea. They're paying full retail price for cereal. A road trip would cost more than you make in a year. Though it'd still be cheaper than a Tesla.

To support those trips, the company builds a network of refueling stations across the country. There are silos of marshmallows to burn as fuel and silos of hard pieces to throw away as garbage. Even cars don't like the crunchy parts.

Amount of Sense Metaphors Make by Length

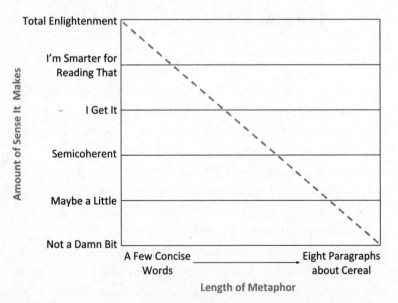

Finally, after years of preparation, the factory builds a car. Yes, *a* car. As in one. Then Tasty Fuel-Os shuts down production and levels the factory so it can never, ever build one again. The only explanation the company gives is, "One was enough."

The decision doesn't make sense. After years of research and grocery shopping, why would the company suddenly call it quits after just one car?

I don't know. Ask a parent who had just one kid.

The Numbers Game

Kids and cars have a lot in common. They're expensive, bad for the environment, and powered mostly by cereal. But above all else, children and automobiles are both easier to produce and maintain after you get set up for the first one. No sane company would build all that infrastructure for just one car; no sane parent would upend their life for just one kid. Although if you ever meet a sane parent, let me know.

As a parent, you finished the research and development phase when you had your first child. You read the pregnancy books, bought all the baby stuff, and learned firsthand what really happens in the delivery room—although you wish you could unlearn it. Or maybe you went through the alternate but equally arduous process of adoption. If you think having your own kid is tough, try having somebody else's. Either way, you paid the costs in terms of time, money, and lost sleep. You might as well get more bang for your buck by building in bulk.

The biggest adjustment in any parent's life is going from zero kids to one. At that point, you switch from only being responsible for yourself to being responsible for another

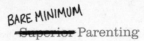
person. And, no, getting a pet isn't the same thing. You can't lock a child in the laundry room while you go out for drinks. Well, you could, but only till your feral laundry child escapes and terrorizes the neighbors.

Going from one kid to two isn't a big deal. It won't disrupt your social calendar. You already spend 99 percent of your free time at home. Plus all your clothes are already stained by various baby fluids, so there's nothing left to ruin. And thanks to your previously crushed spirit, it already seems normal for a tiny human to scream at you. Just sit back and expect more of the same. You'll barely even notice the next kid is there.

But if you do notice them, you'll know what to do. You worked out the kinks on the prototype. If your oldest child is still alive, you were successful at childproofing your house. Whatever's left isn't fatal. It's always the stuff you least expect, anyway. Your kid will be fine around steak knives but cut themselves on a pillowcase. The true curse of the pharaohs is Egyptian cotton.

If you have another kid, you won't waste time sanitizing things. Before the age of five, half of a child's diet is dirt. But you'll no longer cringe by the time kid number two eats food off the floor. You'll just be grateful they didn't get a plate dirty.

Adding another child also won't force you to change vehicles. Anything that can hold one car seat can hold two. Unless you drive your kid around on the back of a motorcycle. Then you won't have time for another child. You'll be too busy collecting trophies for being the coolest parent ever.

As for supplies, you'll still have all the baby gear from your first kid: the fancy stroller that cost as much as your car but was too big to fit inside it; the baby papoose you only used a few times because your kid is a tiny space heater and you kept dripping sweat on them; and all the clothes your kid wore for thirty seconds before they outgrew them. Now all that high-end stuff costs half as much because, by having a second kid, you'll use it twice. Your first kid was full retail price. Your second one is on clearance. By kid number three, someone might as well be paying you. If you get to four, you've basically won the lottery. As a rich parent of four, I promise this is a real thing and not a lie at all.

Financial Impact of Your Life Choices

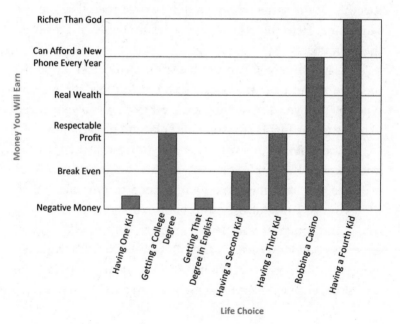

Smarter, Not Harder

Two children aren't twice as much work as one. If you're already yelling at the first kid, just add the name of the second kid at the end. In fact, it's always a good idea to include both names, even if only one kid is in trouble. The other one was probably up to something, too. You'll seem omniscient. In reality, you're just too lazy to separate the innocent from the guilty.

Having a second kid won't double your obligations, either. If the kids are close enough in age, you can drop them off together at the same school and embarrass them both at the same time. Help them beat peer pressure by scaring away all their friends.

To save time, you can double up their doctors' appointments, too. And use the opportunity to find out their blood types. Before you stop having kids, verify that you've secured yourself a reasonable stockpile of replacement kidneys.

Grocery store runs won't take any longer. Just adjust the quantities of the foods you were already buying. If your kids are ages five and under, you won't need to purchase much of anything. They subsist entirely on old Cheerios they find under the couch. If you have teenagers, on the other hand, expect to buy food by the pallet. But time-wise, it's the same stop with the same grocery list and the same coupons. The only difference is, with teenagers you'll need a box truck.

Activities That Are Better with Two Kids Than One

Activity	Advantage of Two Kids
Visiting Grandparents	Kids can evenly divide the awkward small talk.
Swimming Lessons	They'll learn to swim better by trying to drown each other.
Learning to Read	Stolen sibling diaries won't read themselves.
Picking Up	No one cleans faster than two kids hiding the evidence.
Sports	Pointless sibling rivalries promote equally pointless athletic excellence.
Professional Wrestling	You can't have a tag team of one.
Dueling	A sibling makes the perfect second.
Piggyback Rides	Good luck giving one to yourself.

Deceptive Minimum

You're probably very confused right now, and not just because, as a parent, that's your natural state. Shouldn't a bare minimum parent want one kid, the lowest possible number of children after zero? Kids don't come in fractions.

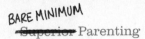
In reality, one kid is more work than any other number of children. With an only child, you'll be their sole source of entertainment. True, there are electronic gadgets and other distractions, but you'll be your kid's only human contact at home. Every time they're bored—which, no matter how many toys they have, will be all the time—they'll come straight to you. You'll have a bull's-eye on your back. Hide someplace with food and booze.

If you have more than one kid, you can make them entertain each other. They might spend every waking second fighting, but it still keeps them busy. Just send them into the yard or a corner of the second floor where you can't hear them. If you notice blood leaking through the ceiling, maybe go check.

Even if you have just one kid yourself, you won't really have just one kid. You'll have somebody else's kid, too. Irritating you might entertain your kid for a while, but eventually they'll want a friend to come over to double the annoyance factor.

And a friend is worse than your own kid. While the visiting child is at your house, you'll have to be on your best behavior. Worse, you'll need to keep your abode reasonably clean and wear pants. Regret feels like tight jeans in the middle of the afternoon.

You'll have to make other special exceptions for the visiting child, too. You can't discipline someone else's kid like you discipline your own. Your kid's friend will have diplomatic immunity. That will embolden your own child, who for the duration of the visit you won't be able to discipline the way you want, either. If the visiting kid goes home and reports that your child spent the entire time in time-out, someone might come over for a well-being check. That's one more time you'd have to clean the house.

This pressure to invite other kids over will be constant. Your child will want to have a friend over on weekends and vacations and the weeknights when they're bored, which will be all of them. Your gut reaction will be to say no, but the word that leaves your mouth will be "yes." Your will is strong, but your guilt is stronger. Your child's loneliness, like everything else in their life, will be your fault.

You'll also feel pressure to have activities planned because somebody else's kid is involved. Your own child already knows you're a disappointment, but when their friend is over, you'll have someone to impress. Going places and doing things flies in the face of everything bare minimum parents stand for. Plus it's expensive. You'll have to pay for yourself, your kid, and your kid's friend everywhere you go. You didn't save money by not having a second kid. You just wasted it on somebody else.

Planned Activities for When Someone Else's Kid Visits

Activity	Pro	Con
Circus	Cheap entertainment.	They won't take your kid, no matter how much you beg.
Professional Sporting Event	Kills three hours.	Kills your budget for three months.

Activity	Pro	Con
Ice Cream Shop	Ice cream.	You'll watch two cones get dropped instead of one.
A Walk	Exercise.	Exercise.
Water Park	You won't have to worry about bathroom breaks.	Neither will anyone else.
Movie	You won't hear either kid over the surround sound.	Popcorn for three will cost a second mortgage.
Campfire	Smoke will drive away bugs.	It won't drive away kids.
Shooting Range	Your kid's friend won't be allowed back.	Might attract doomsday preppers.

Limited Appeal

There might not always be a friend available for your only child. Their pal might have siblings to play with instead. Or they might simply be tired of your kid. You love your child unconditionally, and even you get sick of them.

Making new friends can be hard for an only child. Without siblings to interact with, they'll learn all their early social skills from you. But by the time you become a parent, you'll be done making friends. On most days, the only people you'll see will be coworkers and other parents, neither of which make great additions to your empty social circle. Coworkers are in your life simply because you're paid to coexist in the same unpleasant place, while other parents invite unwanted comparisons to yourself. And you're the one who's supposed to socialize your kid. Good luck.

I'm about to make some sweeping generalizations—as opposed to the rest of this book, which is nothing but sweeping generalizations. Okay, fine. Brace yourself for more of the same. Many only children are great at getting along with adults because that's who they interact with at home. But only children sometimes find interacting with other kids challenging. In their own home, an only child is the center of the universe. They never have to share toys or compete for attention. But other kids won't treat your child that way. Narcissism isn't a team sport.

The great thing about siblings in a multi-child home is your kid can't get rid of them. No matter how awful your children are to each other, they have to stick around and work it out. Through sheer force of proximity, your kids will resolve their issues with each other—and then develop a whole new set of issues to replace them. As a result, your children will be normal, if only in the sense that they'll be just as messed up as everybody else.

But friends have no obligation to stick around when the going gets tough. They can simply cut off all contact with your child before your kid learns how to get along. The only consolation you can give your kid is telling them that eventually their friends would have drifted away anyway. That's sure to make them feel better.

Reasons Friendships Fall Apart

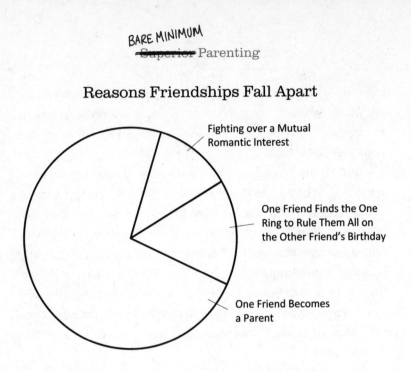

Fighting over a Mutual Romantic Interest

One Friend Finds the One Ring to Rule Them All on the Other Friend's Birthday

One Friend Becomes a Parent

Pressure Cooker

Having only one kid puts more pressure on everyone, including your child. They are the entire next generation of your family. Whether your bloodline continues or dies out forever is all up to them. If they decide not to have kids, they'll voluntarily drive your family name to extinction. Or maybe they'll want kids but can't have them. Either way, if you only have one kid, you'll be overly concerned with the status of your child's reproductive system. That should make for a healthy parent-child relationship.

As a bare minimum parent, you want a return on your investment. Otherwise, why bother raising a kid at all? If your one and only child turns out to be a bust, you wasted eighteen years of your life. Every family has at least one black sheep. If you only have one kid, your odds aren't looking good.

Division of Labor

There are times when having multiple kids can make life harder. When several children team up, there's no limit to the destruction they can cause. That's what happened at Chernobyl.

But there are also times when kids work together to make your life easier. If you have enough children, they'll raise themselves. Like any pack animal, siblings form a hierarchy. Your children will know which kid is in charge and which kid they would eat if it really came down to it. It pays not to be the youngest or the chubbiest.

But there's a trade-off for the power the top sibling enjoys. They're expected to offer their younger brothers and sisters some degree of nurturing and protection, at least when they're not making their lives a living hell. Every group of siblings has one mother hen or, well, I'm not sure what the male equivalent is. "Father cock" sounds wrong. But you get the idea. Siblings step up and look out for each other when necessary. If you're doing the bare minimum amount of parenting, it'll be necessary a lot.

Adding It All Up

Having multiple kids makes it simpler to hit the benchmarks of successful parenting. In a large family, your kids will be used to fending for themselves, so supporting themselves as adults will be an easy transition. Your children will have a hard time being deviants with other kids around to teach them social skills—and to tattle on them when they step out of line. Never underestimate the value of a narc. Best of all, your kids will never blame you for anything. They'll be too busy blaming each other. Congratulations—you raised an entire herd of scapegoats.

If you wanted more kids and couldn't have them, that's fine. Your child will probably still turn out as average as everybody else's. Just know that raising one kid isn't any easier than raising several. Parenting is hard no matter how many children you have. Adding a few more won't make your life any worse when the first kid has already ruined it.

Chapter 7
Space ~~to Thrive~~
Not to Kill Each Other

The hardest part about having multiple kids is figuring out where to put them. You can't leave them out in the yard, and nobody makes an aquarium big enough. It's just as well. You don't want to spend all your free time blowing up floaties.

Inconveniently, kids think their natural habitat is inside your house. In fact, they expect to have the run of the place. Sure, you can confine them to just part of the house when they're young, but that won't last. Things get awkward if you try to stop a teenager with a baby gate.

Despite being small—at least at the start—kids take up a lot of space. The amount of room you need to accommodate their clothes, toys, plates, and other associated gear is inversely proportional to your child's age. A baby needs the most room. Despite their being immobile, you'll need acres of indoor habitat to raise one. A bottle doesn't take up much room by itself, but then you need a bottle sanitizer. And a sanitizer that sanitizes the bottle sanitizer. And the incinerator that destroys all the sanitizers because it's the only way to kill every single germ. A bare minimum parent would never buy those appliances, but you'll probably get them as baby shower gifts anyway. You can't stop capitalism.

As your kid gets older, their stuff will cost more, but it will take up less space. Their flat-panel TV can be mounted on the wall, and their laptop can be closed and tucked away, especially when you walk into the room. I'm sure they were just embarrassed by all the learning they were doing.

As a bare minimum parent, you should give your child the space they need to grow up, but not much more than that. Don't be like overachieving parents, who think a nursery should be big enough to hold a regulation-size tennis court. Square footage isn't cheap, and all that athletic grunting would wake up the baby. Besides, it's dangerous to give children too much room because they grow to fill the size of their container. At least their egos do. Just ask the kid with the six-bedroom house. They're dying to tell you about their weekend in the Hamptons.

Child Personalities by House Size

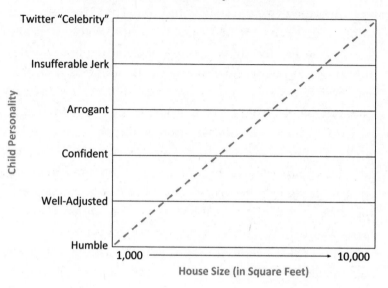

Basic Amenities

What's the best kind of home for raising a kid? Wrong question. It's like you didn't read the title of this book. The right question is, "What's the bare minimum amount of shelter you can get away with?" As with everything else in parenting, the answer is disappointing.

It takes a fair amount of house to raise a kid who won't hate you. And that house must have all the amenities normally expected in Western civilization. If you have twelve bedrooms but your kid has to poop somewhere other than a toilet, that'll definitely be part of their tragic backstory. Pray their memoir doesn't include a chapter titled "The Bucket."

Internet service is also a must. It doesn't matter if you have a picturesque country estate with the perfect tree for a tire swing. If you can't get high-speed internet, you're basically Amish. And no, the dicey country alternatives like satellite internet don't count. Slow internet is the same as no internet. If you have to wait more than two seconds for a website to load, you might as well ask someone to print it out and mail it.

Also keep in mind how any potential home looks, not so much for your kid's sake as for yours. Documentaries about notorious figures always show their childhood home to figure out how things went so wrong. Make sure that home has curb appeal. Your kid might blame you, but the audience won't. Those well-trimmed hedges prove you're not at fault.

Lastly, a safe neighborhood is also a must. Ideally, playing outside shouldn't come with an imminent risk of death. In some areas, that might mean gunshots. In others, it could mean giant eagles. Ever since the war ended, housing prices have been out of control in Middle-earth.

It shouldn't be hard to find a home that meets those criteria. The vast majority of nice-looking houses feature indoor plumbing, internet access, and minimal risk of giant eagle attacks. How, then, should you decide between them? Since you bought this book, I'll help you pick the right place on your first try. The cover price is way cheaper than hiring movers a second time.

Tiny House

As a bare minimum parent, you don't need a McMansion with forty acres of hardwood floors and three bathrooms per family member. Leave that to the overachieving parents and their jumbo mortgages. But you do need something bigger than a tiny house. A tiny house is essentially a trailer home, only a tenth of the size and ten times the cost. I'm sure those tiny custom granite countertops really pop. Most people live in trailers because they're poor. Tiny house owners do it because they feel smugly superior and are bad with money. These are not the kind of people you want as neighbors.

A tiny house might be the bare minimum amount of space you can buy, but it will make your life exponentially more difficult. It's essentially a semi-mobile prison cell that vaguely resembles a real house. In terms of square footage, you'd be better off with an actual prison cell. Those come with a real, working toilet. Tiny homes only have a composting one, which means you haul your poop around with you until you manually dump it. Even prisoners don't have to do that. Plus their stay is free.

Oddly enough, tiny houses appeal to some overachieving parents who think the confined space will bring them closer to their child. And it will. Way, way too close. The good news is they wouldn't be cramped for long. After the first night in a tiny house, one of them would kill the other, and the survivor would move into that sweet prison cell. It's a win-win for everyone, including the dead person. Even hell is better than a tiny house.

Tiny House vs. a Prison Cell

Tiny House	Prison Cell
Not secure.	Safe from break-ins AND breakouts.
You have to buy your own toiletries.	Toilet paper is provided.
You have to find your own roommate.	The state finds one for you.
You have to move it from place to place.	You stay in one spot for decades.
Neighbors can complain about you.	Prison guards are unreceptive to any complaints.
Your house can be repossessed.	You won't be kicked out for any reason.
Annoying friends and relatives can drop by anytime.	Visiting times are extremely limited.
No space for your yoga mat.	Free gym membership and ample time to work out.

Houseboat

If you've ever had neighbors, you recognize the value of a good moat. Other people can't judge you if they drown. Unfortunately, most municipalities frown upon digging a water barrier inside city limits, and besides, moats aren't cheap. They were only economical when they were dug by serfs, whose only payment was the vague promise you'd protect them from

Vikings. And if you didn't, they couldn't complain because they'd be carried off as plunder.

So if you can't bring the water to your home, what should you do? The easy thing: Bring your home to the water. All aboard the houseboat.

Houseboats are bigger than tiny homes but just as mobile. They can float up a river or be cemented in place at a permanent mooring. I recommend the latter. A permanent mooring both stops the house from drifting away and deters sea monster attacks. Keep a broom on the porch to shoo away the kraken.

Houseboats can have internet and plumbing, so they're functional for bare minimum families. Just stay inside. Some older houseboats still flush their toilets directly into the surrounding water, which can put a damper on Marco Polo. Lake parties are more fun without dysentery.

The downside of houseboats is they cause as many problems as they solve. While you won't be bothered by your fellow parents, you'll have other, more nautical challenges to deal with, and those can be even worse. Everyone has a kid who's dumped out the silverware drawer, but few have a kid who sank their house. Just remember the captain shouldn't go down with the ship. No one else wants to raise your kid.

Nautical Terms That Apply to Houseboats

Nautical Term	How It Applies to Houseboats
Poop Deck	The bathroom.
Helm	The remote control.

Nautical Term	How It Applies to Houseboats
Brig	The time-out corner.
Captain's Quarters	Your kid's bedroom. What, you thought you were in charge?
Enemy Fleet	Other houseboats.
Pirate Booty	Torrented adult films.
Anchor	The poor life choices that hold you in place.
Plank	The window you jump out when it all becomes too much.

Apartments, Condos, and Town Houses

For bare minimum parents who are landlocked, apartments, condos, and town houses seem like a passable fit. They're cheaper than stand-alone houses of the same size, and they come with fewer responsibilities. While you're dealing with problems inside—namely, your kid—someone else can deal with problems outside—namely, yard work. Too bad that isn't as great as it sounds. The cost of all that outdoor work is built into your rent or association fees. You could just as easily buy a detached home and pay someone else to do everything outside your house. It's almost like you end up footing the bill no matter what because nothing in life is free. Go figure.

These types of homes are also the opposite of houseboats when it comes to proximity to other people. Your home will be physically attached to your neighbor's, so they'll hear everything your kid says and does. EVERYTHING. Only move into an apartment, condo, or town house if you want to permanently share a wall with people who hate you.

One-Story House

If you're looking for the smallest practical house in which to raise a kid, a one-story house is a passable choice. It's literally the fewest number of stories you can have. Any less and you'd be homeless.

One-story homes are safer than two-story homes. If there's an emergency, you can jump out any window without injuring yourself. Of course, your kid can use those same windows to sneak away. It's up to you if you want to lock the window after they go out.

One-story houses are great for elderly people because they don't have stairs. You might not think you're old yet, but your child will age you prematurely. Besides, stairs take effort, so a second story isn't something you want in your life anyway. Unless you can replace those stairs with an elevator or a firehouse pole. In that case, can I live with you?

Multistory House

A two-story house has approximately twice as many stories as a one-story house, give or take a story. In theory, that's twice as much space to spread out your belongings and feel less cramped. In practice, it's an excuse to get twice as much stuff.

If that doubling includes the number of kids you have, you'll need a four-story house. Adjust your budget accordingly.

Two-story homes offer some options not available in other types of shelter. You can put your master bedroom on the same floor as your kid's bedroom so you can keep an eye on them, or you could put your bedroom on a different floor, giving you more privacy. Warning: Quiet time away from your kid can lead to more kids. There's nothing wrong with that. Just know what you're getting into. And start shopping for that four-story house.

Styles of Houses

Style	Description
Bungalow	Any home bungled by a low-bidding contractor.
Craftsman	Built from craft supplies. Watch out for load-bearing popsicle sticks.
Colonial	Built by a local oppressed population.
Dutch Colonial	Same oppression, but with more tulips.
Cape Cod	Comes standard with a harpoon room for chasing white whales.
Spanish	A regular house with a bullfighting ring.

Mediterranean	Features high, strong walls to keep out marauding Greeks.
Tudor	Can't be in the same neighborhood as Stuart houses.

Shared Space

One determining factor in which type of house you buy will likely be whether or not you want your kid to have their own bedroom. If you only have one kid, that's not a huge issue. You should have more than one bedroom as long as you don't live in an igloo. Although if you do, your walls will melt in the spring, and then your kid will have plenty of space to spread out.

The bedroom debate gets more complicated when you have multiple kids. The crucial factor is age. Babies usually get their own rooms. It's not feasible to fit six metric tons of baby gear and another child in the same ten-foot-by-ten-foot area. And if you do somehow jam two kids in there, one noise from the older kid will wake up the baby. Then one kid will be sleeping in the room and the other will be sleeping in the yard. Serves them right.

When your kids are older, the debate over giving them their own room versus making them share becomes more nuanced. If your kid has to share a room with a sibling, that's fine. If they have to share a room with you, that's less than ideal. If they have to share a room with the car, that's a problem. Trust me, you don't want your kid to sleep in the garage. That's probably

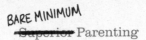
where you keep your power tools. Avoid putting your child out there unless you think your car needs more drill holes.

Personally, I'm a fan of stacking children. Bunk beds let you cram more kids into a small area, which means you can get by in a smaller house with fewer bedrooms. By sleeping in bunk beds, your kids will learn to share a space, and if the one in the top bunk falls out of bed, they'll learn a lesson about gravity they'll always remember—unless they land on their head. Then they'll immediately forget.

If your kid has their own room like overachieving parents suggest, they'll learn a different set of lessons. They'll discover that you're willing to bend over backward to accommodate their needs, at least spatially. Surely they won't abuse that knowledge. They'll also learn how great it is to live alone before they lose that privilege, first by being crammed into a dorm room and later by moving in with a romantic partner. If you don't inoculate your kid against the annoyances of other people by making them share a room, they'll gain antisocial tendencies at an early age. That's fair, though. People are the worst.

Location, Location, Location

Even if you decide each of your children should have their own bedroom, it might not be possible. Your house size is dictated by your budget, and how far that stretches depends on where you live. Money goes further in some places than in others, although it always travels in the same direction: away from you.

Don't live someplace where the price of a house is on par with a lottery win. From a kid's perspective, a house is a house. It doesn't matter if the windows look out over a landfill or an expensive beach where even the surfboards have valet parking. At some point, your kid will put on headphones and ignore the world anyway. You don't need a million-dollar view if all your kid will ever see is a four-inch screen.

The truth is you don't need to live somewhere expensive for your kid to turn out okay. Not that overachieving parents will ever believe that. Super moms and dads think they need a major metropolitan center—and the expenses that come with it—to raise their kid. That's where all the jobs are, right?

Sure. There are no jobs anywhere else in the country. If San Francisco fell into the ocean, the nation's unemployment rate would be 100 percent. Well, that's not quite true. There would be a few jobs for scuba tours of the sunken ruins. Natural disasters aren't so bad as long as you can turn a profit.

I'm going out on a limb here, but maybe—just maybe—there are literally millions of jobs outside the five most expensive metropolitan areas in the country. Yes, the jobs in other places pay less, but it also costs less to live there, so your standard of living will be higher. If you want to live in Silicon Valley, you'll need a thirty-year mortgage just to sleep in a dumpster. And those aren't exactly forgiving jobs. On the bright side, after you work yourself to death, your kid can use your life insurance money to move someplace more reasonable.

Unlike overachieving parents, your aim as a bare minimum mom or dad shouldn't be to land the job that pays the most. It should be to find the job with the greatest asymmetry between how much you get paid and how much it costs to live in the area. You'd be better off with a slightly above-average job in a cheap area than you would be with a high-paying job in an expensive area. Happiness comes from having more than the people around you do. Not so much that you start gloating,

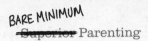

and definitely not so much that your neighbors rob you. But enough that you don't have to be jealous of anybody else. Then you won't be tempted to work harder to get more. You can just keep doing what you're doing now and float through life. Parenting will never be easy, but at least your job can be. Cut your corners before they cut you.

Chapter 8

~~Preserving Perfect Moments~~

Take a Picture— It'll Last Longer

Now that you've attained the bare minimum amount of housing, you have to decorate it. Leaving the walls bare will make it seem like you're not trying. You're not, but it's best not to tip your hand too early. Your kid might take you for granted if they realize how easy this bare minimum parenting gig really is.

Fortunately, sprucing up your walls won't be hard. You walk around with a powerful camera in your pocket, and you live with a tiny human model that you're biologically compelled to think is the cutest thing in the world. Don't deny it. Every parent feels that way about their own child. It's the only reason we don't eat them.

You could do worse than lining your walls with pictures of your kid. Hanging up mirrors, for example. Life is depressing enough without seeing your own face all the time. Printing family photos is also cheap, at least compared to bringing home a Degas or a Monet. And unlike an impressionist painting, pictures of your kid actually look like something. No need to spend a lifetime striving for perfection on canvas when you can pull off photorealism with one click.

Taking pictures of your kid seems straightforward, but as always, overachieving parents ruin it for everyone. Instead of simply hanging their child's photos here or there to make their walls less prison-like, they treat each image like a masterpiece of historic importance. They think their snapshots will be of great interest not just to themselves and their child, but to their children's children and all the generations thereafter. Someday, those photos will stand in a museum, a shining example of a decade or even a century of human history. Their kid will be the sole representative of an entire era, all thanks to their superior photography skills. That's worth bragging about at the weekly mom's group.

These delusions of grandeur put pressure on all parents to act as their child's personal paparazzi. Don't give in. As a bare minimum parent, you should take just enough photos to convince your kid they had a good childhood and then quit while you're ahead. It'll be better for you, better for your kid, and better for future generations. Is there anything laziness can't do?

The Eternal Image

Photography obligations are relatively new. For hundreds of thousands of years, people lived and died without ever creating a single image of themselves. When prehistoric humans did finally get around to drawing people on rock walls, they weren't overly concerned with accuracy. Everybody just looked like blobby stick figures, which wasn't exactly flattering. Everyone knows cave paintings add ten pounds.

Despite these limitations, children thrived. They didn't care if there was no record of their childhood. They just assumed if they weren't eaten by saber-tooth tigers, it must have been pretty good. And even if they weren't convinced their parents raised them right, it didn't matter. Everyone died by the age of twenty. Nothing stops whining like an early death.

Even after artistic techniques improved, childhood milestones still went undocumented. Up through the Renaissance, only the wealthiest aristocrats could commission oil paintings of themselves. Everyone else toiled away in obscurity without any apparent harm. Those commoners who did end up in a painting didn't benefit from it. Nobody wants to be remembered forever as Generic Peasant Number Five.

The idea that childhood needs to be visually documented at all didn't exist until recently. Your great-grandparents didn't have a picture of themselves for every birthday. They're lucky if there's one picture to prove they existed at all. For many of your ancestors, the only sentimental token they left behind was a headstone. Not quite as fun as a picture of a toddler dumping spaghetti. Old people are such buzzkills.

Your great-grandparents survived just fine without childhood pictures—until they eventually died, presumably from causes that were non–picture related. But even if there were a bunch of pictures of them, what would you do with them? You wouldn't hang up baby pics of someone who died before you were born. Best-case scenario, you'd toss them in a box in your attic for a few decades and then take them out for one of those antique appraisal shows. But they wouldn't be worth anything. Nobody else wants pictures of your dead relatives either.

Eventually, the pictures you're taking of your kid now will cause that same problem, only a thousandfold. Three generations down the road, your descendants won't spend hours lovingly browsing through your photo albums. They'll be too busy frantically taking pictures of their own kids—or taking holograms of them if science is finally to that point. And three generations after that, those holographic data cards will be in a box in someone else's forgotten loft space. Pictures don't immortalize anyone; they just force future generations to build bigger attics.

Don't Look Now

Even if your kid someday looks back at their old photos, it won't help them any. Pictures bring nothing but pain. Your child doesn't want their dorky middle-school pictures to see the light of day. Unless they use them as the "before" pictures to show how far they've come. In that case, you're only taking pictures of your kid now so they can look back later and laugh at their own lameness. You're just setting them up to bully themselves in the future. Not your finest moment.

The Most Embarrassing Childhood Pictures

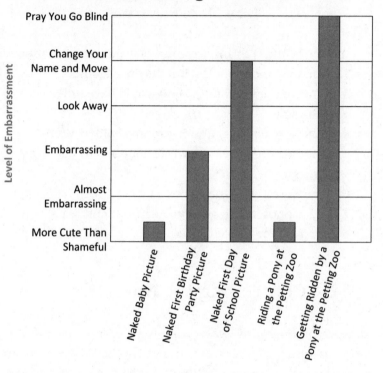

Then again, your kid might instead see an old photo of themselves and realize they look worse now than they did back then, in which case their photo albums are a slideshow of relentless deterioration. Thanks for preserving that pick-me-up.

Either way, photos cause emotional trauma. Take as few as possible. A picture is worth a thousand words, and every one of them is "ouch."

Top Excuses for Why You Didn't Take More Pictures

1. Your child is a vampire and won't show up on camera.
2. You took more photos, but they're classified.
3. Your camera is haunted and would have stolen your kid's soul.
4. You were too busy photographing Spider-Man.
5. Your kid didn't really have a childhood. It was all a dream.
6. The spy satellites beat you to it.
7. Flash photography would burn your child's pale skin.
8. Your phone ran out of film.

Controlling the Narrative

The pre-photography era was a golden age of bare minimum parenting, but it's over now. The world today is an overachiever's paradise built with small cameras and massive hard drives. Parents are expected to document every moment of their child's life with thousands of pictures from sixteen different angles. Don't forget the bird's-eye view. Send up the drone.

Sadly, if you don't take any pictures, you'll immediately miss the third benchmark of successful parenting. Your kid will take one look at the floor-to-ceiling photo mosaics in their friend's house and assume you've neglected them. Maybe you have. Without photographic evidence one way or the other, it's impossible to say for sure. In the eternal blame game of parenting, that's checkmate.

Even as a bare minimum parent, you have to take pictures. Not enough to document every second of your child's waking life—and certainly not as many as overachieving parents—but enough to convince your kid they had a good childhood. It might be a lie, but that's okay because you're the one holding the camera. History is written by the victors. Except in parenting, where it's written by you.

In your child's early life, you are the record keeper. You decide which nine pictures to hang on the wall and which two embarrassing stories to repeat over and over until your kid tells their friends you were eaten by wolves. Don't take it personally. You'll be miraculously regurgitated when your kid needs gas money.

Unexpected Facial Expressions in Photos When You Thought Your Kid Was Smiling

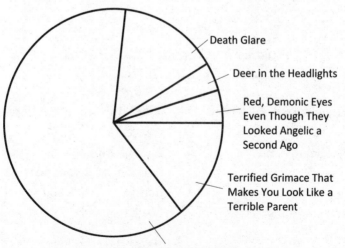

Death Glare

Deer in the Headlights

Red, Demonic Eyes Even Though They Looked Angelic a Second Ago

Terrified Grimace That Makes You Look Like a Terrible Parent

The Urgent Need to Poop

As the sole archivist for those first precious years, it would be unethical for you to skew the historical record in your favor. But you already do it all the time.

Don't deny it. You sift through five hundred vacation photos of your screaming child only to share the one picture where your hell spawn has a goofy smile. Never mind that it was actually a weird split-second half-grimace on the way to a sneeze. You didn't share a memory; you spread a lie. Which is fine as long as it gets plenty of likes.

Someday those photographic falsehoods will trick your kid into believing they had a fun, fulfilling childhood. It's much harder for your child to blame you for their problems if every picture of their early years shows them having the time of their life. They'll never know about the countless pictures you deleted along the way. If childhood photo albums were accurate, they'd be 95 percent temper tantrums and 5 percent naps. Only you couldn't have taken pictures of those because you would've been asleep, too.

Tips for Photographing Children

Tip	Reason
The blurrier, the better.	Hides the disappointment in your child's eyes.
Keep it distant.	Those happy specks on the horizon are someone else's family.
Tell your kids to feign laughter.	Beats real tears.

Promise this is the last picture.	Works ten or twenty times in a row.
Choose black and white over color.	Has fewer shades to show stains.
Shoot in low light.	People will think you're a bad photographer rather than a bad parent.
Offer incentives.	The greatest prize is being done with pictures.

Embracing the Myth

Don't feel guilty for lying with images. In fact, don't feel guilty for anything. You'll ignore that advice, but I had to try.

Nobody shares honest pictures of their kid. If they did, people would stop having children and the human race would go extinct. And you need the human race to continue if you want an easy life. You don't want to generate your own electricity or fix your own furnace or drive your own garbage truck. You need a society full of other people to do those things for you. The older you get, the more you'll need younger people to support you. You better hope the next generation is still going strong when you're too old to wipe your own butt.

But the next generation would never exist if the current generation understood what they were getting into by becoming parents. No rational adult would look at a truthful image of a two-year-old and think, "That's what I want: an enraged mini-human to scream at me." Children are the most effective form of birth control.

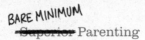
Clearly nothing could be worse than sharing what kids are really like. Thank goodness you've been a liar since birth.

Well, since your child's birth. No matter how excited you were, you didn't post a picture of your infant covered in birthing goo. (That's a technical term. Look it up.) And you certainly didn't share the audio of the delivery room. That's when 90 percent of all swear words are invented. You can't afford those FCC fines. You have a kid.

Instead, on the first day of your child's life, you shared silent pictures of your baby cleaned up and dressed in an adorable little stocking cap. Other potential parents saw that tiny bundle of joy and thought—well, they didn't think anything. They were too busy making babies of their own. Pregnancy is contagious.

By lying about how great your kid's childhood is, you're not just helping yourself; you're also helping mankind. The ripple effect of your lies and the lies of your fellow parents will convince a younger, dumber generation to reproduce as well. Don't apologize. Your dishonesty serves the greater good. If you don't think the perpetuation of the human race is a worthwhile goal, you're rooting for the wrong team. Go be a goat or something.

By using deceptive photography to spark the birth rate, you'll also take the pressure off yourself. You don't want the future of our species to rest on your shoulders. That's overachieving-parent territory. If you hope to get by doing as little as possible, you need as many other people as possible to reproduce. That way if you ruin your kid beyond redemption, there will be better children in other families who can grow up to be functional adults and keep society running. As long as you keep lying with your photos, you'll create other parents whose parenting will then average out your shortcomings. Let somebody else save the human race for a change. You have better things to do.

Behind the Curtain

One caution about deceiving the world with pro-child propaganda: Don't fall for it yourself. You know your life on Facebook is a sham, but the self-doubt inherent in all parents might trick you into thinking other moms and dads are telling the truth. The pictures of their smiling, happy families seem so real. Look at those filters. Valencia wouldn't lie to you.

Come on. Do you honestly think you're the only one being dishonest?

It's arrogant to believe you're uniquely inferior. Much like your child, you're not particularly inventive or special. If you cut a corner, millions of other parents cut it, too. We're all turning squares into circles together.

No matter what the photographic evidence suggests, no kid has ever had a perfect birthday or a perfect Christmas or a perfect anything. People just use captions like that because it's nicer than saying, "After this picture, none of us spoke to each other for two days." "Perfect" isn't bragging; it's a cry for help.

Photo Captions vs. What They Really Mean

Original Caption	What It Really Means
I'm the luckiest parent in the world.	My kid is for sale.
They're so full of energy.	Please, God, make them sleep.
I love coming home to them.	I'm building a secret life in another state.
So much fun.	Kill me now.
We're crazy.	We're so ordinary, it physically hurts.
It's not always easy, but I wouldn't trade it for anything in the world.	I'd trade it for literally anything in the world.
Blessed.	Cursed by a demon with a sick sense of humor.
I just had to share this cute video.	If you look closely, I'm blinking SOS.

See What I Did There?

You want your own kid to look at your pictures so they'll think you did a good job raising them, and you want other adults to look so they have kids of their own. But there's one person who shouldn't view the pictures: you.

After you do the initial editing, you don't have time to dwell on what your kid was like years ago. You're too busy dwelling on the problems they cause right now. Besides, it's insulting to your kid to fixate on their past. "Sure, Son, you're okay now as an investment banker, but I liked you better when you were the third-grade spelling bee champ." At least they can spell "disappointment."

Parents only look back nostalgically if their child is unbearable in the present. But if those old pictures reassure you, you're falling for your own selectively edited fiction. Your kid was always a monster. They just used to be a cuter one.

Your Good Side

Regardless of whether or not you ever look at your kid's picture again, you do need to put enough photos on the walls to convince them they had a great childhood. To pull that off, you don't need a lot of lies. Just a few really good ones for key moments.

Your kid won't remember most of their early years, so only photograph the milestones they'll ask about later. They might not remember their first birthday, but they can reasonably assume they had one. And when they ask, you better have a picture of a fat baby smashing a cake. It doesn't have to be yours, though. Your kid won't know the difference.

There are several other milestones your kid might ask about someday. Save a visual record of the following:

- *Birth*: Every hero needs an origin story. Every middle manager does, too.
- *Eating something messy*: Every kid needs at least one picture of a meal that looks like a murder scene.
- *All the early birthdays*: You'll want to remind your kid of the time when they were too young to be disappointed by your presents. Or your presence.

- *The first day of school*: This used to mean a child's first day of school ever, but now it means the first day of each grade. Thanks, social media. While annoying, taking a picture each year will create a neat flip book that shows the school system slowly breaking your child. There's one for the memory box.
- *Vacation*: Note there's no "s" on the end. Multiple vacations with a child can be fatal. You need one picture to show you attempted to have fun at least once. You'll fail, but no one else will know that once you share that one picture of your kid laughing in delight. Never mind that it's because they were watching you get stung to death by an entire school of jellyfish. You still got the shot.
- *Graduations*: But only the big ones. Graduating high school proves your kid had a pulse. Graduating college proves they had a pulse and a high tolerance for alcohol. Take a picture so you can pretend those two achievements still mean something.

If you neglected any of these milestones, use photo-editing software to fake them. Or say all your family pictures burned up in a fire. Start an actual fire to cover your tracks. You can never be too careful.

Not every missed photo opportunity is arson-worthy. In fact, you should never photograph certain things in the first place:

- *Anything without clothes*: Bath time. Potty training. Bachelor parties. If you take a picture of any of these events, your kid has the legal right to make you eat it.

- *Any "graduation" when your kid is legally too young to drop out of school*: Eighth-grade graduation isn't a real thing. Even if your child flunks a few times, the school will move them up eventually because no one wants a seventeen-year-old hanging out with middle schoolers. Congratulations, your kid advanced because they were creepy. No photos, please.
- *Weddings*: As a parent, you'll have duties at your child's marriage ceremony other than taking pictures. In fact, your kid will pay someone entirely too much to photograph the event. Unless that person is you, turn off your camera.

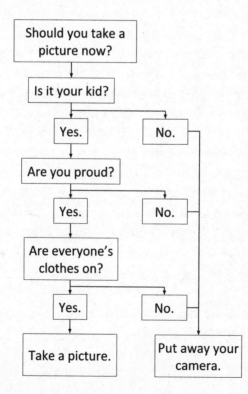

Your child's wedding marks the official end of your photography duties. If your kid never gets married, a good cutoff point is when they have a kid of their own. Once they're busy deflecting blame from their own offspring, you're off the hook.

What if your kid never gets married or reproduces? First, congratulate them for not revisiting your mistakes. Maybe history doesn't have to repeat itself. As for when you should stop taking pictures, your amateur photography sessions have always embarrassed your kid. Stop when they also embarrass you. If your child is in their forties and you take a picture, they better have done something amazing, like cured cancer or eradicated salad.

While you're expected to maintain a photographic record up until those cutoff points, the truth is your kid will have a surplus of their own pictures of themselves as soon as they get a phone. The nine pictures of them on your wall will pale in comparison to the sixty-five selfies they take every time they walk into a bathroom. Future archaeologists will wonder why our most popular photography studios all had sinks and toilets. Maybe it was our religion or something.

Once your child has their own phone, you'll lose control of the historical narrative. Don't panic. This won't prevent you from hitting the no-blame benchmark because there still won't be any evidence about what kind of a parent you were. Your kid will only take pictures of themselves. In the movie of their life, your part will be cut. If you're lucky, they'll leave your name in the credits. Or maybe they'll just replace you with a stunt double.

Playing Favorites

Narrowing down what you consider a photo-worthy moment will be all the more critical if you have multiple kids. You'll have to keep the picture totals for each child exactly equal. Any more or less and you'll be playing favorites. And, yes, your kids will notice—and remember. Pictures may come and go, but sibling rivalry is forever.

Before you take a picture of an event, ask yourself if you want an unbreakable obligation to photograph the same occasion for each subsequent child. Then put your camera down and go find the refreshment table. A good bare minimum parent neglects all their children equally while pillaging the cracker tray.

Wall of Fame

Now that you have a small but respectable collection of childhood propaganda, it's time to display it. Where you showcase your lies is as important as the lies themselves. If you put your kid's soccer photo on the mantel and their graduation photo above the basement stairs, you're telling your kid they were an excellent athlete with a GPA so low it was subterranean. Though if that's the case, your kid won't be insulted. They won't even know what "subterranean" means.

As your child walks by these pictures every day, they'll come to believe them through sheer repetition. Their entire childhood will boil down to whichever mistruths you choose to set above the fireplace. No pressure.

Picture Importance Based on Where It's Placed

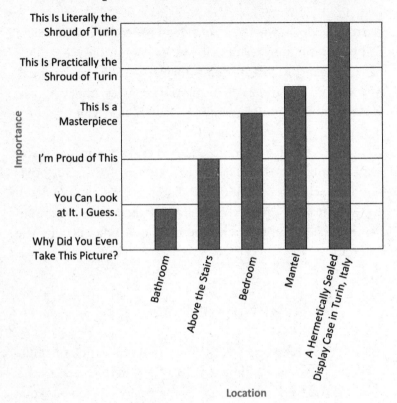

Underneath It All

Your pictures can still help remind you of the truth, even if they never directly capture it. With happy, upbeat images of your kid, the part that's real will be what's just off camera: a toddler crying because the ocean is wet; a high schooler rolling their eyes so hard their retinas detach; a preschooler going to the emergency room for snorting a dime. At least you can put it toward your bill. You'll be proud of these pictures not because of what you caught on camera, but because of what you didn't. Out of sight, out of the historical record forever.

Chapter 9

~~Communication~~

Their Eyes Only

Unfortunately, you aren't the only one in your house who doesn't tell the whole truth. Your kid has secrets. They won't tell you who they have a crush on, where they keep their special rock, or who used your white kitchen towel to wipe mud off their dirt bike. Spoiler alert: It wasn't the dog.

A secret is the first sign your child is their own person with an agenda different from your own. That's a problem for over-achieving parents. One of the main reasons they're obsessed with their kid's "success" is they don't view their child as separate from themselves. Their offspring's triumphs belong to mom and dad, and their failures do, too. Such a kid is more an accessory than an individual, an accent piece intended to make their parents look good. There are cheaper ways to pull that off. Maybe next time just buy a nice purse.

As a bare minimum parent, you shouldn't run into that problem. In fact, you shouldn't run into anything. It's better to walk. If you take credit for everything your kid does, you won't be able to dodge the blame when things go wrong. That's obviously a nonstarter. Instead, keep some distance between yourself and your kid's daily affairs. The more space, the better—probably for them, but definitely for you. And that's what really matters.

With secrets, a child is asserting their right to privacy as an individual. Admittedly, that can be dangerous. Kids are enough of a mystery without deliberate concealment thrown in. When your child is older, they might even engage in disinformation campaigns to throw you off their trail. So much for loyalty. If you wanted a sidekick for life, you should have gotten a dog.

Overachieving parents react to this lack of real information by working harder to find the truth. As always, that's the wrong move. As a bare minimum parent, you should leave your child's secrets alone as long as your kid is still on track to be a functional human being. Don't breach their privacy unless they're doing something dangerous or illegal, like cockfighting or tax fraud. If your basement is covered in rooster blood or fraudulent W-2s, it's time to ask some tough questions.

Dependently Independent

It's easy to see why overachieving parents have a hard time dealing with their child's privacy. Your kid might be a separate person, but it's tough to see them that way when they would literally die without you. You provide them with food, shelter, and clothing, without which they would be in a three-way race to starve, freeze, or get taken down by the police. Law

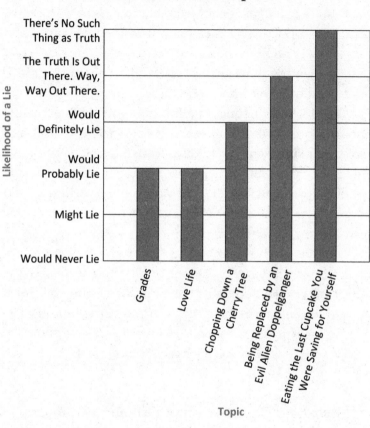

Likelihood Your Kid Will Lie to You on a Given Topic

enforcement doesn't like touching streakers, but that's why God made stun guns.

This helpless stage lasts longer than it should. Your kid will be incapable of using the microwave well into their teenage years. Instead of providing for themselves, they'll sit in a kitchen full of food and complain there's nothing to eat.

Nothing good, at least. Forget hunting and killing their own meal. They're not even capable of boiling ramen.

Despite this dependency, a child is a person with rights, including privacy. It's easier for you in the long run if you respect that and keep yourself selectively ignorant on certain parts of their life. You can't feel guilty about not solving problems you didn't even know were there.

That includes dating. Wading into your kid's romantic entanglements will create years of extra work for you and make your kid resent you for life. Leave them alone as long as you're sure they know the possible consequences. Teenagers could get pregnant, middle schoolers could have drama, and kindergarteners could be asked to share their cookies. Puppy love is no match for Oreos.

Your kid needs to fumble their way through relationships on their own without your intervention. If you give them space, they'll either figure out what they want or give up on human companionship altogether. They can't buy love, but they can adopt it for a modest rehoming fee. Just remember the humane society will cut your kid off after the first dozen cats.

Pros and Cons of Companionship Animals

Animal	Pro	Con
Goose	Mean enough to scare away enemies.	Mean enough to scare away you.
Dog	Would die for you.	Will die before you.
Cat	Has nine lives.	Would watch you die.

Turtle	Can't run away.	Can walk away briskly.
Pig	Super-intelligent animal capable of anything.	Can't trust them after reading *Animal Farm*.
Horse	Can give you a ride.	Hard to take on a plane.
Parrot	Can repeat words and phrases.	Can testify against you in court.
Possum	Has a hidden pocket for extra storage.	You can't tell if it's playing dead or you're a bad pet owner.

Secrets upon Secrets

Most of the information your kid withholds from you will be mundane. They're not afraid to throw up walls of secrecy around unimportant parts of their life. The more trivial, the better. They don't need a reason. Being difficult is its own reward.

Just try asking your kid what they did at school. If you get an answer other than "Nothing," your home must have an interrogation center. That's much more practical than a sunroom. Of course, if someone asks you what you did at work, you might also say "Nothing." Some days are best forgotten.

If you press your child, even a simple story about swapping desserts with another kid will escalate from uninteresting factoid to state secret. That's where overachieving parents fall into a trap. They take this reluctance to divulge information as a clue their child has something worth hiding. They don't,

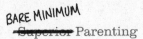

but they'll take any interest from a parent as a cue to hide their pointless secret even harder. They'll die before they tell you the pudding exchange rate. Your kid isn't playing hard-to-get. They're playing impossible-to-live-with.

For a bare minimum parent, this is a welcome shift from your child's early days with language. Every parent spends the first twelve months of their child's life eagerly waiting for their kid to talk and the next three years wishing they'd stop. The question stage is especially rough. For a time, their life is nothing but a series of rapid-fire queries, the answers to which lead to an unending chain of follow-up questions. Why is the sky blue? Why is the dog soft? Why do the faceless children visit me at night? It's best not to answer that last one.

The switch from asking too many questions to avoiding questions completely is sudden. It usually happens when your kid finally does something worth asking about. When they're with you most of the day, you know far too much about their lives. You'll forever remember how they like their sandwiches cut up or what they look like when they're about to poop. It's hard to miss that evil grin.

But as soon as your kid goes to kindergarten, they lose the desire to share information. This is partly because they sense your eagerness. Childhood is one long power trip. But it's also because their feelings about questions change once they're in school. Nothing kills a child's curiosity like learning.

Even if your kid were willing to tell you everything about their life, you wouldn't want to hear it. Their petty dealings aren't much different than your own. Theirs are just with actual children rather than adults who act like them. Your curiosity is only piqued because of the mystery, but just like every book or movie in that genre, the answer is always less interesting than the question. To preserve calm in your life and your child's, agree to a truce where you both acknowledge neither of your lives are worth asking about. Embrace the boring. This is you.

The Book of Non-Secrets

Overachieving parents try to find ways over their child's moat of silence. If your kid doesn't talk, maybe they write. No matter how bland your child's life is, they might still keep a journal. Dry, tedious works land the biggest publishing deals. Just ask the guy who wrote the Bible.

To an overachieving parent, there's no greater temptation than reading their kid's diary. They think a journal is a window into their child's soul rather than a list of toys their kid wants to buy. Yes, there might also be information in there about sleepovers and crushes, but those things don't matter. The likelihood of a relationship lasting from elementary school to adulthood is slim to none. Not many wedding vows start with, "I loved you from the moment I saw you eating glue."

Bare minimum parents know diaries aren't worth reading, but that doesn't mean diaries are harmless. There's always danger with a paper trail. Tell your child not to write anything down if they kill someone. They need to confide in a lawyer, not a book that will be entered into evidence. Also, tell your kid not to record anything they don't want to see in print if they become famous. You don't want your child's unauthorized biography to be titled *Chief Justice: The Bed-Wetting Years.*

The Seal Is Broken

While it's usually best to show as little interest in your child's personal life as possible, there are times when you'll need to violate your kid's privacy. If there's smoke coming out from under their bedroom door, kick it in. Your child is inhaling something illegal or burning down the house. Either way, you have a vested interest in the consequences.

You should also get nosy if you suspect your child is in danger. Overachieving parents abuse this excuse. A sudden change in behavior indicates adolescence, not a life-threatening situation. If every time a teenager acted moody it was because they were in mortal peril, none of them would survive.

Instead, look for concrete signs of a threat before you barge into your kid's personal space. Mysterious pentagrams on the walls, glowing red eyes, or stigmata are all clues it's time to start monitoring their text messages. And, yes, most threats to teenagers are supernatural. Regular mortals are afraid of them.

Not Sharing Is Caring

As a bare minimum parent, you'll have an easier time than most respecting your child's privacy, but your kid might have trouble respecting their own. Rather than withholding their secrets, they might hide the truth by using pictures to lie on the internet. It's the worst-case scenario. They turned out just like you.

In keeping with family tradition, your kid may want to portray their life as being better than it really is. The problem is they have a different definition of "better" than any rational human being. While you use pictures of your kid to portray a lie more wholesome than reality, your kid will create a fake life that's more extreme. That always involves less clothing and more danger than you'd like. On the internet, every high schooler is a seminude party animal. No wonder parents go gray.

This is especially true on the parts of the internet your kid thinks you'll never see. Your child assumes you'll be baffled by anything new enough to be cool. They're not wrong. My grandma still tries to use her cordless phone to turn on the TV. But today's secret apps aren't as hidden as kids think, and the disappearing pictures they send to just one friend have a way of spreading around the world. The second rule of the internet is anything you try to hide will be seen by everyone. The first rule is if you don't have anything nice to say, you'll fit right in.

Just like it's no longer possible to avoid taking pictures of your kid, it's also too late to keep your kid off the internet. At this point, even toasters post status updates. "Burned" is always good for a few likes. You're better off teaching your kid to use the internet responsibly than banning them from it altogether. The harder you try to keep them off of it, the more likely they are to burn toast.

Your duty as a bare minimum parent is just to passively monitor your kid's online activity. Ask yourself two questions about anything they post: (1) Does it show something illegal? (2) Will it create more work for you? The last thing you want is a call from some other kid's angry parent, much less the police. In a few years, there won't even be detectives. A trial will just be a judge slowly scrolling through your kid's Facebook page.

Drama, legal or otherwise, could ruin your child's life—or worse, require you to do stuff. Don't let that happen to you.

Sharing for Life

By respecting your child's privacy except in cases of imminent danger or legal consequences, you'll have an easier relationship with them when they're an adult. If you keep your distance, your child will think you're setting healthy boundaries rather than displaying a general lack of interest in their life. In reality, you're doing both.

This lack of knowledge will also ease your mind. You can't worry about what you don't know. That's a lie. Parents worry about the unknown all the time. But it's different when your kid grows up. At some point, you'll decide you've done a good enough job and your kid can handle life on their own. If your adult child doesn't call for a while, they might just be taking a night class or doing volunteer work. Thinking that is more comforting than knowing they got their hand stuck in a vending machine. Damn those pretzels.

Loose Lips

The world needs more secrets, not fewer. Leave your child's diary alone and don't ask more questions than you have to. The less you know, the less you'll have to do. As for oversharing on the internet, warn your kid about the scary things that could happen. If they post too much, they might get murdered or—worse—turn into a social media star. It's every parent's darkest nightmare.

If you stick to those parameters, you'll hit all three benchmarks of successful parenting without really trying at all. If your kid is used to dealing with their own problems without you butting into their personal life, they'll learn how to take care of themselves. If your kid is used to protecting their secrets, they're less likely to be arrested for being a social deviant. They might still be one, but at least they won't get caught. And if you have no idea what your kid is up to, they can't blame you for their problems. That's a life well lived. Or wishful thinking.

Chapter 10

~~Achieving Peak Academic Performance~~

Schooled

Your kid might never say a word about what they do at school all day, but you still want them to learn as much as possible. All parents agree there's nothing more important than a first-rate education.

Well, almost all parents.

Bare minimum moms and dads think a high-pressure, top-tier education is a waste of time, money, and effort. Don't worry, this isn't an anti-intellectual rant about why you should throw rocks at people who can read. Casting stones at anyone is impolite, and besides, I happen to be literate. Not that you can tell based on this book.

Overachieving parents put education in a category by itself in terms of importance, but its impact averages out over a life-time just like everything else. By the time someone is forty, you can't tell if they went to a run-down school with daily fistfights or a rich school with customized escalators. In the long run, an overachiever's kid at an exclusive school won't be any better off than your kid at an average one, save for a few minor differences. Their kid will always have fresher legs thanks to all those escalators.

How Rich a School Must Be for Amenities

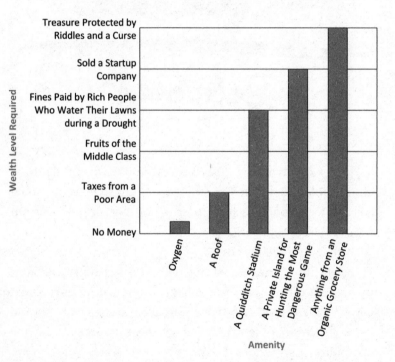

The Price of Excellence

Overachieving parents value education for one reason and one reason only: money. Don't act shocked. Families don't move to the most expensive school district in town to make their child a better poet or a deeper thinker. Overbearing moms and dads think if they spend more money on their kid's education up front, their child will be directly rewarded with a higher pay grade later in life. There's value in a good education, and it starts in the low six figures and comes with a free gym membership and full dental.

Of course, overachieving parents will never say anything that direct. Instead, they claim they want their kid to attend a top-notch school to help them get into a good college. But it's easy to follow that train of thought to its fiery derailment. If you only care about a good education because you want your kid to get into a good college, and if you only want your kid in a good college so they get a good job, and if you only consider a job to be "good" if it has a high salary, then all you really care about is the almighty dollar. Or the almighty pound if you're in the U.K. It's the same overparenting, but with a fancier accent. All that parental concern for your kid—from the day your child got into the best daycare to the day they graduated from the most exclusive college—boils down to shallow materialism. Education is just a long con so your kid can buy stuff.

Overachieving parents deny this money obsession. They claim they just want their kid to be happy, but that excuse doesn't hold up. If happiness were the real goal of education, parents wouldn't obsess over getting their kid into Ivy League schools. Harvard isn't known for producing cheerful graduates, just rich ones. There are dozens of studies on how much graduates earn but none on how much they smile. You can pay off student loans with checks or money orders, but not with a winning grin.

Once an overachiever's kid gets that money, though, it doesn't really help them. They might earn more annually, but they'll waste it on their own kid's future education. Whether it's an overpriced private school or a public school in the most expensive part of town, overachieving parents lock their child into a perpetual cycle of overspending that gets handed down from one generation to the next. But as a bare minimum parent, you can send your kid to a normal school and spend the money you save on beer, and your kids and grandkids can someday do the same. That might not make your family happier, but it will make you drunker, and that's almost the same thing.

Exclusively Nonexclusive

Regardless of whether your kid attends the "best" or "worst" school in the country, the subject matter is the same. Math is still math. Top schools don't have secret knowledge that two plus two actually equals 5.3. They all teach the same mundane trivia that your kid will remember just long enough to pass the test and then purge from their memory forever. It's the only way they'll free up enough space to remember all the Pokémon.

While the subjects are identical, learning them is harder at an elite school, but not in a good way. At an expensive school, your kid will face tougher competition. Rather than fighting for scholarships against kids who spend the day sword-fighting with rulers, they'll compete against the children of doctors and lawyers who are motivated to win. Your kid is better off being the top student at a poor school than the bottom student at a rich one. Especially if you want them to hold their own in a ruler fight.

Overachieving parents will never believe all schools are the same. They'll point out that kids who go to rich high schools get into prestigious colleges. That's true, but not because their kids learned anything special. Rich kids get into rich colleges because they're rich. Overachieving parents aren't getting their kids ahead; they're just paying a premium for mediocrity. Talk about a bad investment.

Differences in How Subjects Are Taught at Poor and Rich Schools

Subject	Poor Schools	Rich Schools
Gym	Dirt track.	Rubber track, and their butlers run for them.
Math	Learn to count on their fingers.	Learn to count with gold coins while laughing at Tiny Tim.
Physics	Limited budget for experiments.	Their lab is Space Camp.
Chemistry	Don't need it because they cook meth.	Don't need it because they buy meth.
English	Learn to write from a workbook.	Learn to hire ghostwriters.
Spanish	Learn to meet new friends in a foreign land.	Learn to talk to the help.

Subject	Poor Schools	Rich Schools
Government	Learn about senators.	Same, but they call them "Mom" and "Dad."
Health	Learn to stay clean.	Learn to avoid poor people.

Learn What Matters

As a bare minimum parent, you shouldn't be concerned about what school your kid attends. Just make sure they learn what they need in order to support themselves and not be a social deviant. There's a close connection between low intelligence and bad behavior. None of the murderous rednecks in *Deliverance* finished high school.

But it doesn't take a top-tier education to prevent your kid from becoming a homicidal hillbilly. Your child can learn to read, write, and do math from any elementary school in the country. Scenic views and state-of-the-art athletic facilities aren't a prerequisite for your kid to spell "cat." Generations of kids mastered all these subjects in one-room schoolhouses with no indoor plumbing or air-conditioning. If you think algebra is hard now, try doing it with heat stroke.

The idea that schools are more or less equal is hard to believe given how closely they're measured and ranked. But all those ratings tell you is what students there are like on average. The stats don't tell you anything about how your individual student would perform. Remember, even at the most prestigious schools, one kid finishes last. And it doesn't bother them at all because they have a trust fund.

Lesson Learned

Wherever your kid goes to school, they'll learn the same fundamental life lessons—and not the ones overachieving parents want to talk about. School will teach your kid that teachers, like everyone else in life, play favorites. Merit matters, but not as much as sucking up. School will also teach your child to jump through hoops to appease an arbitrary, underqualified authority figure who, through a cruel twist of fate, has absolute power over your child's life. But most of all, school will teach your kid to sit still and be bored for hours a day. A student who masters those skills can handle any white-collar job on the planet. Cubicle dwellers aren't born; they're made.

School will also teach your kid valuable lessons about teamwork. On group projects, your child will discover the only thing teammates contribute is dead weight. Plus their names, which partners are happy to add when it's time to take credit. This dynamic remains the same in the working world, but instead of a grade, your kid will get a paycheck. Meanwhile, their useless teammates will get a paycheck AND a promotion. That's called leadership.

Homeschooling

You might be tempted to skip the headaches of the primary and secondary education systems and homeschool your kid instead.

Don't.

First of all, it's too much work. Spending all day, every day with your kid violates everything bare minimum parents stand for. The only thing worse than not spending enough time with your child is spending too much time with them. Just ask your kid.

Second, if you homeschool, there won't be any mitigating influences in their education. Everything will be on you. You can't blame the way your kid turns out on a bad school or a bad teacher. Never underestimate the value of a scapegoat.

Third, there's value to having your kid get roughed up by the system. That's how the real world works. Your child can either single-handedly build a better society, or they can learn to be a well-oiled cog in the machine. One of those outcomes is a lot easier than the other.

Finally, if your kid wants a white-collar job someday, they'll have to join the education system eventually anyway. There's no such thing as homeschooling for college. When your kid starts at a university, it's better for them to have thirteen years of experience with being mistreated by academia than to go in as a rookie. It's dangerous to crush someone's hopes and dreams at such a late stage. Better to do it to them young when it's still okay for them to cry.

The College Difference

But is college even necessary? If you're just trying to turn your kid into a functional adult, a four-year degree seems like over-kill. Your child doesn't need a fancy piece of paper to tell them they're average.

Unfortunately, if you want your kid to get by in society, they'll need a degree, even if it is more work up front. A bache-lor's degree today is like a high school diploma years ago. Your kid can't even bag groceries without a major in food stacking and a minor in crushing the bread with the canned soup. In another decade, they'll need a master's degree to explain the socioeconomic impact of paper versus plastic. And ten years after that, they'll need a doctorate just to walk in the front doors of the grocery store. They might slide open automatically, but not for the uneducated. They can starve.

It's less work for your kid to go to college than to fight the system for their entire life. But that doesn't mean you have to get them into an expensive, exclusive school in a faraway state. A college degree improves your child's job prospects because it shows employers your kid can survive being kicked around by the system for four years. It's good practice for the working world, where your kid will be kicked around for the next four decades.

That piece of paper also shows hiring managers that your kid is normal enough to function in society on at least some level. It might seem like colleges take anyone who can pay, but they do weed out some weirdos. If you have a college degree, an employer can safely assume you can hold a basic conversation and aren't possessed by the devil. Although they might sprinkle you with holy water just in case.

Earning a college degree also shows your kid can make a plan and execute it. Going to college wasn't a good plan. In fact, it was a financially devastating one. But it was a plan nonetheless, and your kid stuck to it. That means something. Namely, that they'll be paying off student loans for the rest of their life.

Above all else, graduating from college shows employers that your kid is desperate. That crushing student debt is a ticking time bomb your kid has to defuse before it blows up their life. Employers know if they make your kid a terrible offer, your kid has to take it. If not, the employer can make an equally terrible offer to the next impoverished graduate while your child starves. Your kid spent four years and all of your money to put themselves at a disadvantage at the bargaining table. College is the most expensive lesson they'll never learn.

Real Knowledge

Beyond those lessons on how to be beaten down by life, most college degrees don't teach usable job skills. All those years studying your major were wasted, just like you usually were. Think about your job right now. Was there anything you learned at college that taught you how to file certain forms or to use a job-specific computer program or to find the best bathroom in which to hide from your boss all day? Probably not. Most accredited universities are woefully understaffed in the hide-and-seek department. When you enter the workforce, you have to be trained or retrained on everything because your job duties have nothing to do with abstract classes like calculus or eighteenth-century French poetry. Unless your job is to teach one of those classes. In that case, I'll pray for you. In English.

Most of the stuff people do day-to-day can be taught in a few weeks or months of on-the-job training. It doesn't really matter if you understand the theories and science behind what you do, because most of your day consists of following the same basic steps over and over again. Push this button. Measure that sample. Put your left foot in and shake it all about. You don't need years of education to do your job. You need a one-page flowchart.

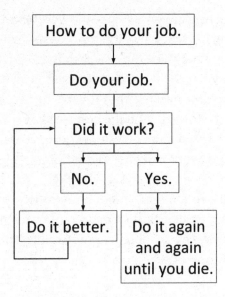

Most of us are production workers, even if we can't see the assembly line. We aren't hired to dream new dreams or develop new ways to do things. If you've ever spent any time around other people, you realize that's for the best. Stupidity is not a recessive trait. The truth is most of us are at work to produce a specific result over and over again, be it a polished widget, a completed file, or an educated student. There's no reason to shell out more for an education just to have your kid turn out just as average as everybody else. It's a lesson rich kids learn the hard way, and they literally pay for it.

School's Out

You can hit all the benchmarks of successful parenting without sending your kid to an elite private school. An ordinary education will prepare your kid for the workforce by mistreating them in all the right ways. It'll stop them from being a social deviant because they'll be too educated to hang out on a river playing a banjo. And it'll prevent your kid from blaming you for their problems because they'll have an entire education system to blame instead. And the best part is you don't have to do anything to reach those milestones. Just make sure your kid gets on the bus every morning and off of it every afternoon. And that second part is optional.

If you stick to a bare minimum education, your kid will turn out fine, just like all the children of overachieving parents. And that will make those parents furious. There's no better reward in the world.

Chapter 11

~~The Path to Athletic Glory~~

Benched

Sadly, overzealous moms and dads don't give up easily. If they can't get an edge for their kid through academia, they'll try for one through sports.

They're not alone.

I did sports. My family did sports. My friends did sports. My enemies did, too. There are more of them, so that's a better sample size. In fact, I don't know a single person who's never done a sport. We all thought it was a good idea.

And we were all wrong.

There's nothing more dangerous than youth sports. I don't mean for your kid. Concussions and broken bones might smart a bit, but that's life. Walk it off, buttercup.

The real danger sports pose is to you, the parent on the sideline. Kids will only damage their bodies and minds. You could lose your immortal soul. When you see your child out there on the field, you'll be tempted to relive your own failed dreams of athletic glory. Don't. Down that road lies effort, and that's the path to the dark side.

To be a bare minimum parent, you must resist the urge to care about sports. Indifference is stronger than love or even the Force. Let your kid join a team if they really want to, but don't encourage them too much. Buy them the required equipment. Pick them up and drop them off. Clap. But the second you switch from passive supporter to diehard fan, you become a sports parent. Enjoy your red lightsaber.

The competitive pull of youth sports is hard to resist. Deep down, we all have a primal urge to see our child do better than other people's kids. It's the ultimate secondhand validation. If your kid wins, that means you're better than those other parents, or at least that you passed on better genes. Whatever it was, your kid triumphed because of you. Brag about it to everyone you know. That never gets old.

It sounds absurd, but otherwise rational people consistently slip into this mind-set when the starting whistle blows. Look around at any sporting event. You might be happy your kid finally kicked the ball in the right direction, but next to you there's probably another parent screaming for their four-year-old to do a slide tackle. Spoiler alert: Preschoolers don't care if they make it to the World Cup. Their only goal is to make it to their halftime juice box.

Few people realize when they cross the line between reasonable human being and sports parent, mostly because they're too busy shouting their heads off about something on the field. The first sign things have gone awry is you think yelling makes a difference. High-decibel parenting won't turn your child into a professional athlete. Neither will screaming at the ref for failing to recognize your child is the second coming of Jesus. The son of God was a great religious figure and an even better goalkeeper. Jesus saves.

Shouting at the top of your lungs isn't even the right way to express your displeasure with a sports official. If someone makes a decision you don't like, here are the proper steps to chew them out:

1. Don't.

It's really that simple. No baseball player has ever made it into the Hall of Fame and said, "I wouldn't be here if my mom didn't make that Little League umpire cry." Professional players would never resort to something so dishonorable. They stick to steroids.

What Sports Parents Yell at Refs vs. What They Mean

What They Say	What They Mean
You suck!	Why am I like this?
Are you blind?!	I shudder when I see myself in the mirror.
Let's take this outside!	I've never satisfied anyone in the bedroom.
What game are you watching?!	I hope it's not the one where I'm making a jackass of myself.
Did the other team pay you?!	I hope so, because you don't make enough money to put up with this kind of verbal abuse.

What They Say	What They Mean
My kid was robbed!	Of a decent childhood by my behavior today.

Reach for the Stars

If you can't shout your kid to greatness, how will they reach the big leagues?

Here's a dirty little secret: They won't. Your kid isn't going to make it in the NFL. Or in the NBA, WNBA, or MLB for that matter. I think America has a professional soccer league now. Your child won't make that one, either. In fact, toss together any sports-related acronym you want. Your kid won't make the cut. Not even in curling.

Don't get mad at me. I did you a favor. Your kid was going to get rejected anyway, but only after you wasted your money and their childhood in a vain attempt to turn them into the superhuman athlete you always wanted to be. It's more economical to have your vicarious sports dreams crushed by a seventeen-dollar book. I might not have all the answers, but I can give you disappointment at a discount.

There's nothing wrong with not achieving greatness at sports—or greatness at anything else, for that matter. As I've made clear from the beginning, we're all headed for mediocrity. Some people just waste time and effort struggling against the inevitable. Spare your kid years of heartbreak and let them be average from the get-go. All those extra coaching sessions are leading right back to the middle with the rest of us.

But how can I be certain of your child's destiny with ordinariness? For starters, you're reading this chapter.

Truly committed sports parents don't need a guide. They already know how to hit it big. They would have made it themselves had they not been sidetracked by some unfair circumstance—a vindictive coach, an untimely injury, or a total lack of any athletic ability whatsoever. That last one is what got me. It's weird how a lifetime of being bad at everything can sneak up on you.

But while sports parents know everything there is to know about succeeding as an athlete, none of them agree on how to pull it off. There's more than one way to ruin a childhood. To sports parents, steamrolling their child's youth will be worth it when their kid hoists whatever arbitrary medal or trophy now defines that kid's entire existence. Ultimately, sports parents just want their kid to have fun—as long as they win or die trying.

There are three unreasonable goals a sports parent uses to wreck their child's life: the Olympics, professional sports, and college athletics. As a bare minimum parent, you'll be surrounded by moms and dads madly chasing these misguided dreams. If you're not careful, you'll get infected, too—if you aren't already. If you ever see your kid make a great play and think, "With a little additional training, they could go far," leave the premises immediately. Then sit your kid in front of the TV. It could take months or years of inaction to save them.

The Easy Way Out

You probably have some doubts right now. At first glance, it seems like the lazy—and thus right—thing to do would be to let your kid excel at sports on their own, then freeload off their success. Isn't that what bare minimum parenting is all about?

Sadly, that shortcut doesn't exist. You might as well declare you're going to save time on your commute by riding down the freeway on a unicorn. That's obviously impossible because (1) unicorns don't exist, and (2) if they did, it would be too hard to attach a license plate. Good luck finding a screw hole.

The naturally gifted child athlete is just as fictional as that unicorn. Every kid starts at the same basic athletic level, with slight variations. Children who are a hair better or older than average tempt their parents into giving them more attention, and so begins the slide down the slippery slope to extra training. Gradually, the normal kids with normal skill levels drift out of sports and lead normal, productive lives. But the kids who showed a mild aptitude and got extra coaching from their parents have to endure years of exhausting, thankless toil before they crash and burn their way out of sports altogether. Those tragic "Where are they now?" documentaries have to come from somewhere.

And, yes, crashing and burning is inevitable. I understand your kid is special, but they're competing against millions of other equally special kids in a race to see who can waste their youth the fastest. When it comes to sports, it really doesn't matter if your child finishes first or last; everyone is a loser.

You no doubt have dozens of counterarguments right now. Nice try. This is a book, not a dialogue. Instead, here's an in-depth look at the Olympics, professional sports, and college athletics to explain why I'm right.

Professional Amateurs

For sports parents who want to turn their kid into a worldwide superstar as quickly as possible, the Olympics are a tempting option. They generally have lower age limits, which is great if you want to put the pressure of international competition on a kid who can't even think about driver's ed without having a panic attack. The Olympics are also the fastest path to the cover of a cereal box. There's no higher honor than to have your picture awkwardly stare at people while they eat their breakfast.

Too bad that dream is already out of reach. If you're reading this and your child is older than a fetus, it's too late for them to qualify for the Olympics. Parents of top gymnasts and swimmers enroll their kids in Soviet-style sports gulags the second they leave the womb. Athletes, like Jedi, start their training young. If your kindergartener doesn't already have their own strength and conditioning coach, they'll never win a gold medal or blow up a Death Star.

Sure, Olympic personnel don't call their training facilities sports gulags, but only because communist punishment methods scare away sponsors. To avoid negative publicity, sports parents use words like "camp" or "homeschool." The latter is technically true. Training for the Olympics for sixteen hours a day counts as an education because the kids learn valuable life lessons, like win or you don't eat. Hunger is an excellent teacher.

The bottom line is kids don't just roll out of bed and pull off world-record swimming times or gymnastics scores. Instead, they give up their entire childhoods to achieve greatness at those arbitrary scoring metrics. As opposed to normal childhoods, which are dedicated to different but equally arbitrary scoring metrics. Those Scantron tests won't fill out themselves.

Even if the impossible happens and your child takes home the gold, it won't be worth it. A typical winner snaps up a few short-term endorsement deals that peter out before the next Olympics. You can't expect the public to remember who your child is for a full four years. This is the Age of the Internet, when fifteen minutes of fame have been reduced to 280 characters. The best your child can hope for is to live on forever in an insulting Olympic meme. It's our version of the pyramids.

A former Olympic athlete's best option is to snag a job as a coach or commentator. Otherwise their skills will become useless as soon as the Olympics end. When else will a world record in the fifty-meter butterfly come in handy? "That guy is drowning! Quick, somebody cross that short body of water in the least efficient way possible!" I'll wait for a boat.

Keep in mind that the past-their-prime child athletes I'm describing here are the "successes." There are only three medals in each event. For every other Olympic athlete around the world who didn't stand on the podium, the years they spent in the sport were a total bust. All they have to show for giving up their childhoods are lingering injuries and the faint echo of the pity clap. The worst part is many of them are too young to drink, so they have to deal with their failure sober.

Still, people who go to the Olympics and fail on the world's largest stage are lucky compared to the people who don't make the team. For every gymnast who qualifies for the final squad, there are dozens more who put in the same hours and didn't even get to be an alternate. Don't be jealous your kid isn't an

Olympic gold medalist; be grateful they aren't an Olympic near miss.

If you're a bare minimum parent, you shouldn't touch Olympic training with a ten-foot pole. Unless you use that pole to pull your kid out of the training pool. If they swim like me, they could use the help.

So what should you do if your child says they want to be an Olympic athlete? Here's a sample conversation:

KID: *I want to be an Olympic swimmer.*
PARENT: *No.*

Then buy them ice cream. Ice cream fixes everything. Note: This also works on adults.

Pros and Cons of Olympic Sports

Sport	Pro	Con
Snowboarding	Will get your kid outside in the winter.	As soon as you put on all their snow gear, they'll need to go to the bathroom.
Sprinting	Will build up your kid's cardio.	You'll never catch them when they're in trouble.
Swimming	Trains your kid not to drown.	You might have to fight off frisky dolphins.

Sport	Pro	Con
Decathlon	Favors kids who are mediocre at many things rather than great at one.	Gives your kid ten times the opportunities for failure with only one medal at stake.
Pole Vault	It's fun to fly through the air.	Practices will turn into jousting matches.
Discus	Makes your kid strong.	Is basically a deadly game of Frisbee.
Cycling	Your kid rides a bike anyway.	Tight shorts eliminate the possibility of future grandchildren.
Javelin	Teaches your kid to throw sharp objects.	No.

Going Pro

The Olympics have one downside even sports parents recognize: They only pay off once every four years. Moms and dads who want to mooch off their kid more consistently steer them toward professional sports. Unlike the Olympics, which shroud the selfish pursuit of individual glory in a thin veneer of patriotism, professional sports are only about earning cold, hard cash. I don't mean literally, of course. Unless you live in Minneapolis or Green Bay, where your child could very well be paid with a wad of frozen bills.

Professional sports certainly seem tempting on the surface. They generate the kind of money that could let your kid support you for the rest of forever. A little effort training your kid up front is okay if it lets you retire twenty years early, right?

Wrong. Maybe you should stop answering my rhetorical questions.

Let's look at the best-case scenario. If by some miracle your overparenting lands your child on a professional team, your kid will be thrown to the wolves—metaphorically for now, but maybe literally in the future. The NFL is always looking for ways to make draft day more exciting.

Think about all the bad decisions you've made in your own life with an ordinary income and no fame whatsoever. Now multiply that by 10,000. That's what your child will be up against. And, no, you won't be able to help them. You're the one who got them into this mess in the first place. Save your tips for when they want to ruin your grandchildren.

Too bad your kid has zero chance of faring well at the professional-sports lifestyle on their own. Take someone in their late teens or early twenties and give them unlimited sex and money. Then put them on national TV any given Sunday. It sounds like a twisted social experiment, not a viable career path. At least they let the guinea pigs wear helmets.

Your kid will wreck their life in record time, but they won't be entirely to blame. You'll be right there with them, encouraging questionable choices that directly benefit you. After all, you gave up so much to force your kid to fulfill your dreams for you. It's only fair that they repay you with a new house and a vacation house and a vacation house from the vacation house for when the other two houses are being cleaned. If your kid really loved you, they could afford all those things. Maybe they should play better.

Money problems are tough, but they won't kill your child. Game days will take care of that. If your kid is a football player, they'll destroy their body day in and day out to make the rich guy who owns the whole operation slightly richer. It's like being a coal miner, but with longer hours and tighter pants.

Football's power to destroy athletes isn't unique. It's just the best reported. Until recently, no one knew about the hidden dangers of concussions. Similar chronic health threats likely lurk beneath the surface of other sports. Rest assured some researcher will eventually prove light jogging causes cancer and tennis makes your genitals explode. I don't know, I'm not a doctor. But whatever your kid is doing now that you think makes them healthier, you can bet someone later on will prove it's actually killing them. Staying out of sports altogether is the safest play. Laziness is the first step toward immortality.

Professional sports will leave your child financially broke and physically broken, but things can still get worse. Whatever is left of your child's traumatized brain will still understand the intense, unrelenting criticism from fans and the press. Every failure will be replayed dozens of times on a giant stadium screen and on millions of TVs around the world. No pressure.

For Olympic athletes, the press takes it easy. Yes, that gymnast failed at their big jump, but they're just a kid and have a bright future ahead of them. But if a professional athlete drops a ball, they've committed an unforgivable crime. In three states, unforced errors are punishable by flogging.

As a society, we've agreed that getting a ball across a line or through a hoop is the apex of human achievement. If our country placed as much emphasis on science and medicine as it does on sports, we'd have a cure for exploding genital syndrome. Until that day, I'll keep wearing my awareness ribbon.

As a bare minimum parent, you know that pushing your kid toward professional sports is a mistake. Even if they succeed as a paid athlete, they'll fail at life. At least they can't blame you for your role in it. After the first few tackles, they won't remember who you are.

Pros and Cons of Professional Sports

Sport	Pro	Con
Football	It's one hell of a ride.	It'll be in a wheelchair.
Baseball	It has more games in a season than any other sport.	You'll work so many days, you might as well get a regular job.
Basketball	It's always indoors.	You must be tall enough to hit your head on everything.
Soccer	All you need is a ball and some grass.	And a corrupt governing body ready to accept millions in bribes.
Hockey	It's fast and fluid.	If it's too fluid, players will drown.

Sport	Pro	Con
Horse Racing	Horses do all the work.	Horses can't pay gambling debts.
Mixed Martial Arts	It's exciting.	Sibling fights just got a lot more deadly.
Auto Racing	You compete sitting down.	It's just a three-hour car trip with no bathroom breaks.

Pay to Play

Not everyone is comfortable sacrificing their kid in such a blatant cash grab. Some sports parents simply want their child to land a full-ride scholarship to college. These moms and dads don't expect to earn a bunch of money for themselves. They just want to get out of paying a bunch of money for their kid. It's the same basic greed, but it's tax deductible. Isn't it okay to push your kid in sports in the name of education?

This might shock you, but the answer to that rhetorical question is once again "no." Who could have foreseen this completely predictable series of events? Don't answer that.

The problem with college scholarships is that otherwise intelligent people forget that nothing is really free. Paying for an education is like any other large purchase, such as a car or a home. Under normal circumstances, you would save up money until you could afford it, or take out a loan and pay it back slowly over time. Or default along with millions of other people to crash the housing market. It's up to you.

But with college, there's another payment option where your child attends for free but in return owes the college four years of indentured servitude. Parents think this is the deal of a lifetime because they don't have to spend their own money. All it costs is a substantial chunk of their child's life. It's a steal, but only because the college is robbing your child blind.

People only fall for this logic when it applies to college. If a bakery offered your child a cookie for zero dollars but in return your kid had to work at the bakery for four years without getting paid, you wouldn't call that cookie "free." Yet for some reason, the parents of college athletes act like their kid won the lottery. In reality, their child was given an education of a set dollar value in exchange for years of physical labor. That's not a prize; it's a job.

As far as careers go, it's one of the worst-paying ones on the planet. When you imagine scholarships, coaches want you to think of ten or fifteen hours of training a week in exchange for a full ride. But in reality, most kids get far less money in exchange for far more time. Even unpopular collegiate sports like swimming and running require several hours of daily training, including during "breaks." Sure, your coach is supposed to give you days off, but that rule means as much as a high school love note. If you believe it, you're only going to get hurt.

Sports are the only things in the universe besides black holes that can literally destroy time. Outside of practices—both legal and illegal—your child will have to go to meetings, attend banquets, show up at team-building events, visit the personal trainer for sports-related injuries, and travel to games, wherever in the world they might be. Since most major universities aren't exactly next-door neighbors, college athletes can kiss their weekends good-bye as they travel across the country to compete. None of those extra hours ever factor into coach math, which is like real math except that it's an outright lie.

It's a good thing those kids don't have anything besides sports on their schedule. But wait: At some—but certainly not all—schools, student athletes must go to class. This is a gross injustice since becoming a better-educated human being won't make your kid a better lacrosse player, but rules are rules. Coaches talk about how being a student is more import-ant than being an athlete, but it doesn't play out that way. Being a mediocre student will keep your kid on the team, but being a mediocre athlete could cost them their scholarship. The only thing more embarrassing than having a bad job is getting fired from it.

At least that would spare your kid from the unpaid over-time. If you tally how many hours your child actually works for their athletic scholarship, they would be better off flipping burgers. They would be safer, too. Your kid would trade the immediate danger of sudden injury for the distant danger of clogged arteries. Bon appétit.

As bad as college athletics are financially, they're still an improvement on your child's earlier years. To even earn the lowly job of college athlete, your kid has to put in thousands of hours at their sport for free. Well, not really for free. As the parent of an athlete, you have to pay for signup fees, equipment, sports camps, gas, and hotel rooms, so your child actually earns negative money. Remind me not to ask you for stock tips.

Scholarships aren't free money that falls from the sky. They're a fractional reimbursement of the money you dumped into your child's amateur sports career. Spending money on your child to win a scholarship is like putting $100 into a claw machine to win a two-dollar stuffed animal. Although that teddy bear might still be worth more than a liberal arts degree.

Some parents are so desperate to get any return on the entire sports debacle that they'll gladly sign up their child for four years of hard labor and poverty. For many student athletes, colleges are just modern-day debtors' prisons, but with more beer and better fight songs.

Unfortunately, alcohol and school spirit don't make for accurate memories. Years later, former student athletes who have never considered the full cost of sports to themselves or their parents will look back fondly on their collegiate careers. Your kid will probably even push their own children to follow in their footsteps. The only thing worse than a bad investment is a bad investment repeated for multiple generations. There's a fine line between school pride and Stockholm syndrome.

Keep It Local

But what about local sports? If your aspirations for your child begin and end in a youth league, there must be some benefit to them. That's why people play them, right?

Nope.

People play sports because everybody else plays sports. And everybody else plays sports because nobody learned their lesson from the people before them. The one thing kids should learn—to quit before they start—is the one sports will never teach them.

Instead, organized athletics teach your child to buy into the weird authoritarian relationship that only exists between an athlete and a coach. "Follow orders so you get more playing time" might not be the lesson you want your kid to learn, unless you hope they'll grow up to be a stormtrooper. Some kids look good in white.

Athletics also teach your kid they have no right to their own time. Without consulting you or your child, coaches and athletic directors schedule mandatory practices and games that your kid must attend—or else. Good luck keeping your child on the basketball team if they take a personal day. They have to be there every second of every practice and game to earn the privilege of continuing to be there for every second of every practice and game. Are we having fun yet?

And woe is your kid if they get hurt. At a real job, if your child gets injured, they get to stay home on paid leave. But in sports, your kid will ride the bus to the away games anyway. Coaches say they're teaching kids to support the team, but what they're really doing is showing them there's no escape. Even the military doesn't work that way. When a soldier gets wounded, nobody sends them back to the front lines to clap for the other troops.

As for the social benefits of sports, your child doesn't need teammates to make friends. Most squads have ten or twelve kids. Without them, your child could befriend a few of the other seven billion people on earth. My kids can't walk from the slide to the monkey bars without making sixteen new friends. Thank goodness that ability fades with age. That much human contact would kill me.

If the only way your child can make friends is through sports, they have bigger problems than the next home game. Most athletic careers are finished by the end of high school. Your kid has a rough adulthood ahead of them if they can only connect with people by playing with a ball or running in big circles. From a social standpoint, they're basically just a golden retriever. Teach them to sit.

Total Commitment

"So what if sports have no benefit?" you say to yourself, since you're talking to a book with no ears. "My kid loves them."

And they do—for a while. At first, kids love sports because they're fun. Then they love them because they're good at them. And finally they love them because if they admit they don't, you'll murder them. After you spend a month's salary on free-throw camp, your child is pretty much locked into basketball for life.

What youth sports really teach kids is to stick with something they hate because their own goals aren't as important as other people's. What you wanted was a well-rounded human being, but what you got was a martyr. Expect that to come up down the road six eggnogs into Christmas.

Every kid follows this sports arc from enthusiasm to self-loathing, so it's no use warning them. Your child will still join a team. If there's one thing kids love, it's being peer-pressured into bad decisions.

The best way to stop your kid from doing sports is to do nothing to stop them. Don't ban them, but don't help them or push them harder. Just give them nominal support until they lose interest and wash out on their own. The worst possible thing you can do is force them to stick with it just because you've already wasted a lot of money. It's always better to cut your losses than to throw good money after bad. Support your kid's decision to quit while staying vague about your real feelings. Save the champagne for after they go to bed. If your child fails as an athlete, you've succeeded as a parent.

If, on the other hand, you actively stop your kid from participating, you'll be vilified for the rest of your life. The world is full of would-be quarterbacks who were one unsigned permission slip away from a Super Bowl. Fortunately, there's no reason to crush your child's dreams. Life will do that for them.

Bulletin Board Material

By not pushing your kid in sports, you'll be better positioned to hit the benchmarks for successful parenting. Your kid will have free time to get a job since they won't be wasting hours a night on practices and games that cost you money. They won't be pushed toward social deviance by a sports culture that values physical prowess over being a decent human being. And they won't blame you for their problems since you'll empower them to escape sports, the biggest problem of all. Congratulations, you have a functional human being on your hands. Now you can both be out of shape together.

If you're a sports parent, don't take all this as a personal attack on you. I'm not here to destroy your life. You're doing a good enough job of that on your own. I'm merely trying to give you the greatest gift one parent can bestow upon another: your weekends back.

If that doesn't make you feel better, don't bother sending me hate mail. If you want to become a true bare minimum parent, you need to stop caring what other people say, including me. Use what advice you can and ignore the rest.

Unless you ignore the advice in that sentence, too. Then I can't help you.

It's never too late to care less. Even if your kid is mid-season, you can always just stop showing up. This doesn't just apply to sports. When you don't show up for their extracurriculars, everybody wins. Especially you.

Chapter 12

~~Perfect~~ Attendance
Imperfect

It's the championship match of the quiz bowl tournament, and your kid's team is behind with one last chance to take the lead. It all comes down to this final question:

"What's the capital of Mexico?"

Both teams smash their buzzers, but your kid's thumb is the fastest. Those thousands of hours of video games paid off after all. And to think, your spouse wanted you to buy your kid books.

All your child has to do is answer this one simple question to win the match, the tournament, and everlasting glory. This is a moment they'll share with their grandchildren. Somebody better take a picture.

Your kid pauses for a second to let the tension build, then proudly blurts out their answer:

"Santa Fe."

"Uh, no," says the moderator. The crowd gasps. Your kid gave the capital for NEW Mexico. The capital of old Mexico is Mexico City. Its founders weren't very creative at naming things. They were too busy inventing tequila.

As your child stares at the floor in disbelief, the other team buzzes in and wins the match. Your kid's teammates look away from your child in stunned silence. This is the worst moment of your kid's life. They embarrassed their friends. They embarrassed their school. They embarrassed themselves.

But they didn't embarrass you. You weren't even there.

And THAT is why your kid missed the question.

Not because of their lack of interest in geography or how poorly they do under pressure or those thousands of hours they spent playing Xbox instead of practicing trivia.

No. They lost because of you. You. You. You. You. You.

Sound delusional? Welcome to the mind of an overachieving parent.

Always There for Them

The truth is even if you had been in the audience to support your kid, nothing would have changed. Your child still would have missed the question—unless you gave them the answer telepathically or blinked it to them in Morse code. Maybe next time your kid could just study more. Yeah, that sounds easier.

It's bad enough that parents enroll their kids in a million activities. But somewhere along the line, it became mandatory for moms and dads to attend those activities, too. That punishes adults and kids alike, but it hasn't stopped overachieving parents from doing it anyway. Then they complain that they never have free time. It's almost like there's a cause-and-effect

The Size of Your Child's Problems

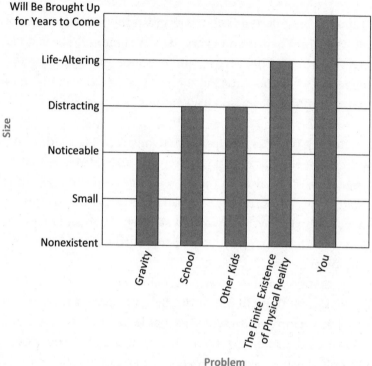

relationship. Who knows? I'll leave that one for scientists to figure out.

My position on sports also applies to all nonathletic activities: You have to pretend to be on board with your kid's participation until they wise up and quit on their own. But that doesn't mean you have to attend every single thing your kid does. Skip your child's events in the right way at the right times to ensure your presence is felt and your absence is never noticed. Be a ninja of nonattendance. Make an impact and then vanish without a trace.

The Power of Presence

Overachieving parents will never grasp the simple joy of not showing up. They attend every activity their child ever does, except for bathroom breaks, and even then there are exceptions. But what about the kid themselves? Do they really want their parents at all six hundred of their weekly events?

Probably.

But not because it helps them in any way. Your kid simply wants to be the center of your attention all the time no matter what. One of the first complete sentences any child learns is "Watch this." Unfortunately, it takes many more years before they finally do anything worth watching. We're all born with an attention-whore gene. Some people grow out of it. The rest join social media.

Is giving your child attention really that bad? Yes. It's literally the worst thing in the world. Better luck next time, raisin cookies. Feeding your child's insatiable lust for attention will get them hooked on external validation. They'll do their best, but only if you're watching from the stands. Otherwise they'll melt into a puddle of unmotivated failure. The only thing worse than a selfish teammate is a liquid one.

Your presence at an event shouldn't make your kid perform better or worse. If it does, you have a problem. Actually, your kid has a problem. You just have the kid, which is like having a million problems at once.

It's best if you can break your child's attention addiction sooner rather than later. There will come a point when you can't be present to support your kid even if you want to. You won't be there to clap during their first job interview or when they ask their boss for a raise or when they propose to their romantic partner. I say "can't," but I should amend that to "shouldn't." I'm sure some overachieving parent hid in the bushes or behind a water cooler and watched all those events. If you know them, please give them this book.

Supporting your kid unconditionally won't make them a strong, independent leader; it'll make them totally dependent on you. What starts with you attending every trivia match will end with you and your adult child living together in a creepy house above your murder motel. Never go into business with family.

That's what your kid can look forward to long term, even if in the short term your child seems to succeed under your loving spectation. Hooked on your attention, your kid will throw themselves passionately into whatever event you're watching. But you're not leading them toward future greatness. You're helping them peak in high school. At least murder motels don't require a college degree.

The Benefits and Drawbacks of Attending Your Kid's Different Milestones

Milestone	Pro	Con
Birthday Party	Hard not to attend. It's in your house.	Equally hard to get out of cleanup.
Making It to State in a Competition	Win or lose, you still love your kid.	Win or lose, you wasted your weekend.

Milestone	Pro	Con
Prom	As a chaperone, you can keep your kid safe.	As a chaperone, you'll be bored and sober.
High School Graduation	Ends one life stage.	Starts a more expensive one.
Wedding	You'll give away your kid.	When the bill comes, you'll give away your retirement fund.
Job Interview	You'll show your kid you support them.	You'll convince the boss not to hire them.
Buying a House	You'll see your kid grow up before your very eyes.	You'll have to help them move.

The Upside of Being Ignored

Overachieving parents say they don't want their kids to be self-centered egomaniacs, but then they turn around and make attending their child's functions their top priority. A kid with that kind of support can be anything they want—except a tolerable human being. If you want to clear a room fast, let the child of perfect-attendance parents talk about themselves. They're the best at everything except humility.

Think about the "horrible" lessons your kid might learn if you miss some of their activities:

1.   They're not the center of the universe.

2. They need to respect other people's schedules.
3. High school events aren't the pinnacle of human achievement.

Someone who learns those lessons is at risk of growing up to be a well-adjusted adult. What would the neighbors think?

A kid's constant need for affirmation is a different kind of attention deficit disorder. And it's your focus, not your child's, that gets called into question. The cure is to wean them off your attention slowly or, better yet, not to get them addicted in the first place. Limit your attendance from the start, and make sure the clubs and sports they join are things they still want to do when you're not looking. If they spend an entire

Amount of Attention Kids Need at Every Age

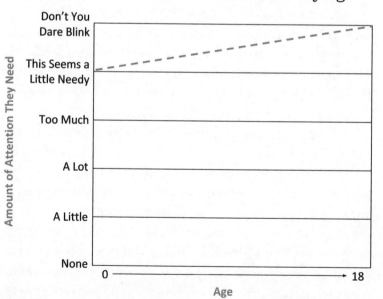

game in your absence picking grass in the outfield, you don't have an athlete, but you might have a landscaper. Congratulations, your yard will look amazing.

The Sixth Man

If you skip all your child's activities, your kid is certain to blame you later in life for their long string of failed relationships. They're never too young to learn to be flaky. So show up. Sometimes. Depending on how far away the game is and whether or not you have a plausible excuse. Job duties are a valid reason not to go. So is important yard work. Cleaning out your backlog of unwatched shows, not so much. Unless those shows are about job stuff or important yard work. Then you hit the slacker jackpot.

What you can and can't skip depends on the frequency of the event. If it only happens once or twice a year, you're stuck. If it happens every weekend, you have some wiggle room. And if it happens every night, you better not attend unless you're at a truly bad place in your life. At that point, you either love the event or hate yourself. Probably both.

So let's say the event is pretty frequent. How do you decide which ones to skip?

First, remember nobody is keeping an attendance log for you, not even your kid. Sure, they'll end up with a general impression of whether you were usually there or not, but in the long run they won't remember specific events any more than you do. Think about your own childhood. If you were like most kids, you had hundreds of activities you wanted your parents to watch. How many of those do you remember?

Probably just the ones where something unusually good or bad happened. Ordinary events with unremarkable outcomes blend into the background. But no one forgets the time they tore a groin muscle at their violin concert. Next time, just take a bow, don't do the splits.

For parents, there's no award for perfect attendance. Even if there were, I'd tell you not to go for it. The true prize for a bare minimum parent is extra free time, not a full trophy case. So how do you maximize your visibility at these events while minimizing the time you waste there?

In true bare minimum fashion, I recommend going for quality over quantity. Rather than attending all twenty events in a season, go to the six or seven most important ones. Unless your kid is really bad. Then attend the ones that are likely to be blowouts so the coach will put your kid in the game. It doesn't matter if it's a lopsided win or a crushing loss. If you're there when your kid gets to play, it counts as good parenting. It also counts if you watch them stay on the bench, but that's not as special. You can watch them sit around at home.

After one event a year, take your kid out for pizza. That'll be the event they remember. Food trumps sports. Unless your kid was doing a musical or something. Then food trumps culture.

Try to do this the final game or performance of the season. There's only one last event each year, so your kid won't expect special food all the time. If you disregard that advice and take your kid out to eat after a random event in the middle of the season, they'll ask you to do it all the time. A poorly timed restaurant trip will only make them whine more. If that was your goal, mission accomplished. Celebrate by buying earplugs.

Best Rewards for a Job Well Done

Reward	Pro	Con
Participation Trophy	Kid feels good about themselves.	They shouldn't.
Trophy They Actually Won	Rewards merit.	Punishes laziness.
Applause	Instant validation.	If your kid doesn't get it next time, instant disappointment.
Money	Turns your child into a capitalist.	Turns their extracurricular activity into a job.
Time Off Practice	Practice is terrible.	It will seem twice as bad when they finally go back.
A Trip	Promotes experiences over things.	Family vacations are a punishment.
A Nap	Pure bliss.	Only works for adults.
Food	The ultimate incentive.	You could have eaten it yourself.

Even if you convince your kid you were usually in the stands, your work still isn't done. You also need to convince other parents. I know, I know, I wrote an entire chapter about ignoring parental peer pressure. But in this case, there's a practical value to making other parents notice you. Unless you plan on committing any crimes. Then stay in the background and keep wearing that fake mustache.

But assuming you're on the straight and narrow, you need to show up to your kid's events enough to be recognizable. Not so much that other parents feel like they can come up to you and start a conversation. That would be tragic. But you need to show up enough that other parents know which kid is yours. That cuts down on the likelihood of your child being kidnapped by a stranger. It also prevents some nosy parent from asking your child why you're never there. You don't need other parents filling your kid's head with doubts. Your child will have a lifetime to do that to themselves.

Scheduling Conflict

You can mitigate most of these dilemmas by not signing your kid up for activities in the first place. If you don't take the initiative and enroll them, chances are they won't even know an activity exists—at least until years later, when it's too late for them to start from scratch. The next time you don't feel like going to a recital, just remember no kid has ever signed themselves up for piano lessons. Your misfortune is self-inflicted. Karma is loud and always misses F sharp.

Exercise this veto of omission with caution. You don't want your kid to resent you for holding them back. It's better to let them find out for themselves how much they hate having eight things to attend every night of their lives. It should take about a week. Doing stuff is the worst.

Underbooked

Selectively skipping your kid's events is good for you and even better for your child. If your child isn't the center of your attention all the time, they're less likely to be a social deviant. Breaking the law isn't as fun if nobody notices. And when all your kid remembers from their extracurricular activities is that one time you bought them deep dish, they won't have a reason to blame you for all the problems in their life. Faulty memories for the win.

As a bare minimum parent, you can still enjoy sitting in the stands at your kid's events. Just make sure those activities aren't the center of your life. A little loving neglect will give your child perspective. The best life lessons are the ones you can teach without leaving home.

But some parents are afraid to let their kid naturally drift away from organized activities. They envision a terrifying future where their child runs amok in their house, unhindered by commitments elsewhere. Fortunately, there's something that stops your kid from running, amok or otherwise, and you have it in your house right now. No, it's not a tranquilizer gun (although that works, too). It's a screen.

Chapter 13

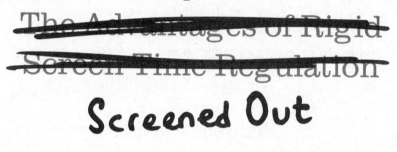

~~The Advantages of Rigid Screen Time Regulation~~

Screened Out

There's nothing more evil than a screen.

Every modern serial killer has watched television at least once. They probably looked at a computer screen, too. Hell, they even may have used a screen door. And don't get me started on sunscreen. Have you ever seen a serial killer with a sunburn?

You don't need to be a homicidal maniac to recognize the danger of screens. Everything bad shows up on them. Violence. Nudity. Work. That last one always gets me. I can walk away from *The Naked Murder Show*, but work emails follow me to the bathroom.

Today, it's in vogue for overachieving parents to limit screen time for their kid. After all, who would want all the information in the world at their child's fingertips when they could make their kid go outside and play with sticks? That should boost their IQ.

To the surprise of no one, I don't buy into the hysteria about screen time. Screens aren't the source of all evil. That honor goes to haunted pet cemeteries or maybe the ocean. I forget where Cthulhu lives. Screens are tools. Wield them wisely and you can slay boredom and keep your child occupied with minimal effort. But limit screen time and you'll have to work harder than ever to fend off anarchy. Banning screens won't lead to a happier home. It'll lead to a nervous breakdown.

Fighting Inertia

One of the main reasons overachieving parents despise screens is that screens contribute to laziness. Not their own, mind you. That would be admirable, and there's nothing to look up to about overachievers. Instead, overbearing moms and dads ban screen time to make their kids more active. They must have a death wish.

The greatest challenge in all of parenting is to get your kid to sit still and shut up. Screens accomplish that. They tether your child to one place with their warm, indifferent glow. It's the only thing that will ever get your kid's full attention. You can tell them a million times to pick up their dirty socks and they won't remember, but they'll hear a toy commercial jingle once and hum it for the rest of their life. That's why educational TV is such a brilliant idea. Too bad kids put it in the same mental category as dirty socks.

Noneducational TV Shows That Are Actually Educational

Show Genre	Pro	Con
Police Procedurals	Teach your kid how to get away with murder.	The victim might be you.
Infomercials	Teach your child about supply and demand.	Your credit card might mysteriously go missing.
Sitcoms	Show your kid anyone can be funny.	If they have a team of writers and a laugh track.
Reality TV	Tells your child anyone can be famous.	Fifteen minutes costs a lifetime of dignity.
News	Shows your kid what the world is really like.	Too scary for children. And for adults.
Cartoons	Give your child a break from reality.	Your child seldom visits reality in the first place.
Soap Operas	Remind your kid that even as people enter and leave the picture, the story line of life is continuous.	Give your kid unrealistic expectations about evil twins and comas.

Show Genre	Pro	Con
Ghost-Hunting Shows	Introduce your child to a world of fascinating mysteries.	Teach your child that while they may never find what they're looking for, they can still land a TV deal.

Even if you don't approve of what TV teaches your kid, at least it keeps them from destroying your house. A child can't both memorize every commercial *and* smash your valuables. Shattering glass drowns out the good parts. Unless your TV has surround sound. Then you're in trouble.

Don't worry about your child getting hyper later. Kids don't save up energy when they watch TV. Looking at screens is exhausting, but you know that firsthand. After a hard day in front of a screen at work, you don't hit the gym. You go home and sit around in front of a screen some more. Behold the power of screens.

Banning your kid from screen time is dangerous, especially when they're home all day. Your child will have all the energy screens were supposed to suck away and more free time than they know what to do with. Your kid won't magically become a better child without screens, just a less distracted one. They'll use their newfound focus to make your life miserable. Don't ask questions about the footprints on the ceiling. Just get a stepladder and a mop.

Where Kids Focus Their Energy in the Absence of Screen Time

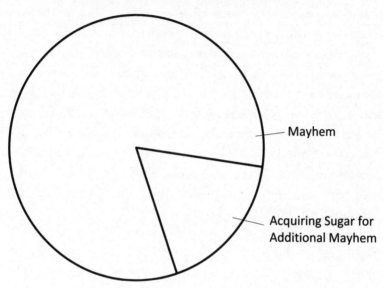

Mayhem

Acquiring Sugar for
Additional Mayhem

What Comes Out

Overachieving parents fear screen time will do more than immobilize their kid. They think it will brainwash them. Screens will take their innocent, impressionable child and reprogram them into a violent, over-sexualized monster. That sounds like something straight out of science fiction. Someone's been watching too much TV.

It's impossible to make a blanket value judgment about screen time. The fact that something is on a screen doesn't make it good or bad, just visible. The world is a scary place, and, no, you can't screen it out. Eventually your child will have to deal with it on their own. If you want your kid to be a functional adult someday, it's better to expose them to it gradually through screens so they won't be blindsided by it all at once. You don't want them to discover sex exists on the day they move out. They might drop a couch or something.

Violence shown on screens worries overachieving parents just as much as sex does. They think exposing their kid to cruelty will desensitize them to it or, worse, make them cruel. That fear is backed up by science. When cartoon characters first dropped anvils on each other, real-life anvil murders skyrocketed 10,000 percent. The same was true for falling pianos and discarded banana peels. Every one of those deaths was confirmed in official records, but historians mistakenly attributed them to World War II.

None of those things are true. But even if they were, that would be all the more reason to let your kid watch violent shows. If cartoons turn other kids into psychopaths, your kid needs to understand what they're up against. Then your child can practice the steps to avoid falling anvils. It's the only reason anyone takes ballet.

Fears about the corrupting influence of television date back to its invention, but admittedly, things have become more graphic since then. Early shows weren't even in color, so no one was traumatized by the triple murder on *Leave It to Beaver*. For all the audience knew, the Cleaver family was gushing maple syrup.

Audiences today don't have that luxury. Now the gore is rendered in high definition in more colors than are visible to the human eye. Not only can you tell it's blood, but you can decipher what type. Usually it's O positive. You can tell by the platelets.

Real-Life Deaths Inspired by Cartoon Violence

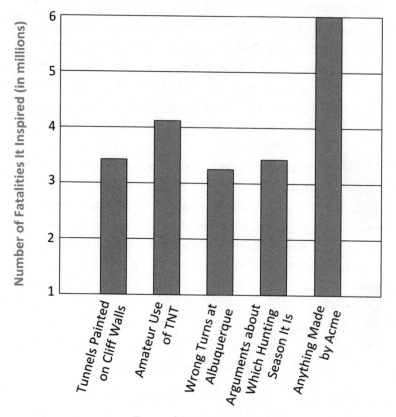

At first glance, it's understandable why an overachieving parent wouldn't want their kid exposed to that. Assuming TV doesn't turn your kid into a serial killer—and the jury is literally still out on that in half a dozen different murder trials—at the very least, violent shows expose your kid to a world more violent than real life. TV murder shows outnumber real-life murders one hundred to one. If there were that many homicides in real life, TV ratings would plummet. No one would be left alive to watch.

But this hyperviolence is a benefit, not a drawback. TV is exaggerated reality. If your kid learns to cope with its more horrifying version of the world, the actual world won't seem so bad by comparison. A desensitized child will grow into a functional adult who can handle anything life throws at them. TV did your job for you. There's nothing more bare minimum than that.

Honestly, most kids aren't that scared of TV violence in the first place. Their actual fears are more common and far more terrifying. When I was in school, 100 percent of my nightmares were about taking a pop quiz. Nobody ever suggested I cope with that fear by dropping out of school. I don't know why turning off the TV to deal with TV-related fears would be any different. My kids might be traumatized, but they won't be quitters.

Scariest Nightmares

Nightmare	Why It's Scary
Falling	Your floor is a mess.
Running from an Unknown Monster	The real terror is cardio.
Getting Chased by a Clown	Their makeup could have been tested on animals.
A Family Member Dying	Like you have room in your schedule for a funeral.

Realizing You're Naked in Front of Your Class	It's cold.
Being Paralyzed	Not moving is only fun when you do it by choice.
Suffocating	It might not be a dream. Maybe someone had enough of your snoring.
You Were Awake the Whole Time	Your life is the nightmare.

Play It Again

If overachieving parents dislike TV, they HATE video games. To them, the violence on a PlayStation or an Xbox is a million times worse because their kid is an active participant, not a passive observer. But video games aren't about violence; they're about problem solving. In this particular case, your kid just solves their problems by shooting them or blowing them up. It's just a Sudoku puzzle with more blood splatter.

Overachieving parents are squeamish about video games because they don't want their kid to literally kill their problems. They fear those glorified murder simulators will turn their child into a murderer in real life. But bare minimum parents know the evidence doesn't bear that out. Hundreds of millions of people have played violent video games. If games that feature killing actually turned people into killers, we'd all be dead. The fact that you're reading this sentence proves video games have yet to drive humanity to extinction. There's always next year.

Somehow we resist digital violence's corrupting influence in real life despite it cropping up in unexpected places. Even in seemingly innocent *Tetris*, the player destroys poor, defenseless blocks row by row. But to date, I've never dealt with other people by dropping them from the air to make them disappear. I've also never tried to kill someone by jumping on their head, or eaten random mushrooms in the hope of growing to twice my size. It helps that I'm a picky eater.

If you sit back and allow your kid to play video games, your child will learn valuable lessons you won't have to teach them later on. For example, at some point, your kid needs to recognize the difference between fantasy and reality. That was easier to do when I was a kid because one was made of eight pixels and the other existed in three dimensions. Today, some video games look better than I do. They certainly have a better frame rate. Discerning fact from fiction is a vital skill your kid should practice early on. Otherwise your child might grow up to believe everything they read on the internet or see on TV. There's a reason some parents think vaccines turn kids into werewolves. To be fair, that's as likely as a shot giving them autism.

Video games can even save your home. Kids are naturally destructive. Rather than having them test your new weed whacker on your bedsheets, let them test a machine gun on digitally rendered demons. One of those targets needs to be destroyed more than the other. Plus, if you ban your kid from that video game, you'll teach them they SHOULDN'T kill the temporal army of the damned. Talk about a mixed message. Any video game can be educational if it teaches your kid to save the world. Mankind will thank you.

Life Lessons Video Games Teach Your Kid

Concept	Lesson
Respawning	Hinduism was right.
Health Packs	Medical care is free and strewn about the ground in unlikely locations.
Difficulty Levels	When the going gets tough, pick an easier setting.
Platforming	The higher you climb, the farther you plummet. Turn off the fall damage.
Dialogue	Always skip the small talk.
Leveling Up	Doing the same boring task over and over makes you more powerful. Warn the guy in the next cubicle.
Cheat Codes	Playing fair is just another way of losing.
Final Boss	Watch your supervisor. Find their weakness. Destroy them.

Read It and Weep

Overachieving parents love working harder than everybody else to give their kid an advantage, even if it only exists in their heads. They can't fathom a world where children succeed at life just by having fun watching TV or playing video games. To

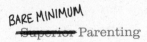

a normal parent, that sounds like a delightful childhood. To an overachieving parent, it's the apocalypse.

To compensate, overachieving parents ban screen time and make their kids read books instead. In case there was any confusion, a book is a lot like the thing you're holding in your hands right now, only it contributes something of value to society—allegedly.

The problem with choosing books over screens is that, in practice, books can be every bit as explicit as TV shows and video games. It's the same content, but displayed on dead trees instead of dead pixels. Except that sometimes books ARE made out of pixels. That's right, books can be on the very same screens overachieving parents curse as the root of all evil. You can read e-books on phones, tablets, computer monitors, smart watches, microwave timers, and virtually anything else with a digital display. Okay, a few of those might not be possible yet, but give it a few years. Soon your bathroom scale will tell you that you need to lose five pounds and read the next chapter of *Great Expectations*. Don't expect a great day either way.

Still, many overachieving parents give books a pass, regardless of what the words in them actually say. For some reason, watching a TV show about a war is bad but reading a book about a war is good. Those moms and dads assume books are beneficial for their kid simply because they're books. That's like assuming poison ivy is good for your child just because it's a plant.

There's nothing inherently good or wholesome about books. Most of the movies and TV shows overachieving parents don't want their kid to watch are based on them. There are no new ideas in Hollywood, or anywhere else for that matter. The original bare minimum parenting book was written in ancient

Mesopotamia, and all it said was don't let your kid get eaten by dragons. Back then, I would've been an awesome parent.

Forcing your kid to view something in their imagination doesn't make it less violent. If their imagination is anything like mine, it will make the brutality go up. As soon as I graduated past picture books—it was last Tuesday—I was free to imagine characters and their worlds however I wanted. Sure, authors describe what things look like, but I'm good at reading between the lines. Remember when James wore robotic armor on that giant peach? You know, to fight off the dinosaur ghosts. No wonder that book won so many awards.

Any parent who assumes a child's mind is a safe, disciplined space has forgotten their own childhood. Kids imagine monsters in every dark space and body of water. There's a reason toddlers are terrified of the toilet. Kids evolved to be cautious as a survival instinct. Children who spent their time cowering in caves lived longer than the ones who played pin the tail on the prehistoric lion. Your kid is biologically programmed to see the world as scarier than it really is. If you make them view stories in their imagination rather than on a screen, they'll sleep in your bed until they're twenty.

Think about it. Everything your kid reads in a book or sees on TV or encounters in a video game was once part of someone else's imagination. It's just been toned down to be suitable for mass consumption. At least when your kid watches a cartoon or plays a first-person shooter, you can see what they see to make sure it's appropriate. When they read a book, all kinds of messed-up stuff could be going on in their head and you would never know it. That innocent children's story just became rated R. In the wrong hands, even Dr. Seuss can be pornographic. Six sick chicks tock, indeed.

Back to the Source

Trying to ban content you don't like is futile, anyway. Even if you succeed under your roof, your kid will just enjoy it somewhere else. You can block channels and websites in your own home, but you can't block them from the entire world—at least not without serious hacking skills. Don't learn to code. Cyber terrorism exceeds the scope of bare minimum parenting.

When your kid leaves your house, they're out of your jurisdiction, no matter how much you want them to believe otherwise. You can't always see what they're doing. You're a parent, not Santa. Everyone knows he died childless.

And, no, it's not some other parent's job to enforce your overly strict screen time limits. If you're the one who made your kid functionally Amish, the burden of keeping them that way is on you. Other parents only have to stick to the bans that keep your kid from dying. A peanut moratorium is worth upholding. A TV ban is not. Unless there's a commercial about peanuts. Then I have no idea what to do.

Letting kids watch banned content when they visit your house isn't the same as letting kids drink alcohol at your house because otherwise they'll do it someplace else. Underage drinking leads to criminal charges and lawsuits, and defending against those is a lot of work.

Screens are legal, and there's no escaping them. The last isolated village in the Amazon has been contacted by text message, and the peak of Mount Everest has free Wi-Fi. You can't send your child to some other parent's house and expect your kid not to watch TV. The other parent will need screen time more than ever to control their suddenly larger herd. In fact, that other mom or dad is doing you a favor. By keeping your kid sedentary with screens, they're preventing your child from racking up damages you would've been liable for. Nobody wants their kid to come home with a $10,000 bill for a destroyed china cabinet. That's a lot to pay for one child-free afternoon.

Annual Damages Kids Cause at Other People's Houses

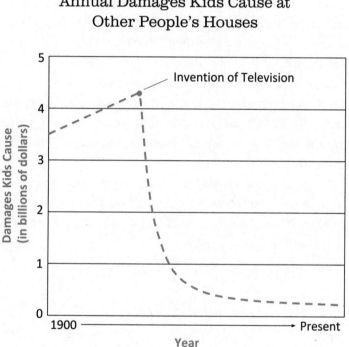

Screens for Everyone

Used correctly, screens will help you hit the three benchmarks of successful parenting with bare minimum effort. A child who's been desensitized by screens will be more prepared for the workforce. If they can handle a documentary about serial killers, they can handle having their will to live murdered every day in a cubicle. At the same time, screens will make your kid less likely to be a serial killer or any other type of social deviant. They'll commit their crimes vicariously through characters on TV or in video games. And if they do happen to take a more active role, they'll at least know how to get away with it thanks to all those crime shows. Best of all, they won't blame you for anything. They'll be distracted from their problems by watching TV.

So let your kid use screens as much as they want. No matter how objectionable the content, letting your kid sit quietly in front of a TV will always be less dangerous than having them roam the house in search of other sources of fun. And that's what really matters.

But what about when screens fail? If your child gets bored with their devices, there's another method you can use to keep your kid in line, though it won't be pleasant for you or them. Exactly like the rest of parenting.

Chapter 14
Rules Are Rules
(Unless They're Hard to Enforce)

Kids are jerks and do bad things. Everybody knows that. Yet if you don't discipline them, people will blame you for all the bad stuff they do anyway. Nobody will give you or your child the benefit of the doubt. That garage didn't burn itself down. Unless it's a coincidence your kid smells like lighter fluid.

For whatever reason, parent shaming is intensely concentrated in the area of discipline. If your kid does poorly in school, no one will say you're a bad tutor. If your kid is afraid of the dark, no one will say you're a substandard monster-killer. But if your kid destroys the garage in a firestorm worthy of the Pacific Theater, suddenly it's your fault for being too soft. Apparently a longer time-out would've been the difference between good behavior and arson. Now you know.

The Most Devastating Fires in History

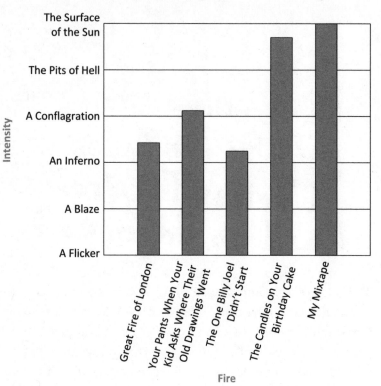

While bare minimum moms and dads shrug off that kind of parent shaming, overachieving parents cannot. To them, everything their child does—their successes, their failures, their misguided experiments with combustible material—belongs to mom and dad. A misbehaving child makes the whole family look bad, and that burns more than a thousand garage fires. Children are supposed to be trainable. If you can teach a dog not to pee in the house, surely you can train a kid not to start a fire in a detached garage.

Except raising a child is less like training man's best friend and more like herding angry bulls. You'll never stop them, but maybe you can poke them with a sharp stick to make them rampage in a different direction. Just steer them down the path where they'll cause the least damage and try not to get trampled. Oh, and invest in a good carpet cleaner.

Once you accept that you'll never have a well-behaved child, the aims of bare minimum discipline become clearer. Get your kid to respect the rules enough that they can hold down a job someday. Prevent their youthful indiscretions from sparking a life of crime. And apply just enough discipline that, if their life goes up in flames, you're protected from blame. Ultimately, the goal of bare minimum discipline isn't to change your child's behavior. It's to make it seem like you're trying. You don't want your adult child to be able to say they have a criminal record because you let them get away with murder. If your kid asks you to help them move a body, politely decline. You have back problems.

As long as you make an effort to discipline your child—even if it's a bare minimum one—you can claim that nothing that happens afterward is your fault. When other parents look at you askew after yet another mysterious garage fire, you can shrug and say, "I sort of tried." Then you're off the hook.

The Penalty Box

If you want to maximize the illusion of discipline while minimizing effort, start with a time-out. Moms and dads have used this tactic for thousands of years, though with mixed results. Philip II of Macedon once put his son Alexander in time-out for taking a toy. Alexander reacted by taking most of Asia. But Mahatma Gandhi's parents also put their son in time-out, and he grew up to be one of the most selfless people ever to live. I'm guessing in both these cases, but I've never heard of a child NOT having a time-out, so the odds are on my side. If you have evidence to the contrary, don't tell my publisher.

The biggest flaw with time-outs is they depend on the honor system. After you put your kid on a chair in the corner, they have to stay there of their own free will. If they get up, the whole system collapses. You can't give them a second time-out. They'll just keep walking away until you end up hyperventilating by yourself in the dark. When you're a parent, every closet is a panic room.

But don't schedule that crying session just yet. As a last resort, you can try these tricks to keep your kid in place and make them think you're trying:

- *Vague threats*: Promise something worse will happen if your kid doesn't stay in the time-out chair. They don't know what that something is, and neither do you. Then hope the fear of the unknown will keep them from calling your bluff.
- *An obstacle course*: Take the scattered debris your child left around the house and use it to surround the chair. The resulting defensive berm could stop a tank.
- *Rope*: I think this is illegal. That's usually the case with things that work.
- *The Tom Sawyer*: Convince your kid it's fun to sit in the time-out chair. Although if it's fun, it defeats the purpose of the punishment. Scratch that plan.

- *Checkout time*: Give yourself a time-out. It won't teach your kid anything, but it's a great chance for you to take a nap. Why punish your kid when you can reward yourself instead?

All of these approaches require at least some work from you, except the nap one. You can do that one in your sleep. But if you prefer a lazier approach (and if you don't, you're most of the way through the wrong book), you might try this next method.

Go Away

You can't always focus on the long game. Yes, you want to use discipline to make your child a better-behaved human being. But sometimes the best you can hope for is to put out fires. Literally. There won't be a garage left standing by the end of this chapter.

If you just want to solve the immediate problem, eliminate its source: your child. I don't mean kill them. You've put in too much work to simply throw it all away like that, even doing the bare minimum. But you can remove your child from the picture for a while. Out of sight, out of mind, out of range of nearby carports.

Rather than corralling your child in a corner, banish them to their room. You can't stop them from being bad, but you can make them go be bad somewhere else. You want discipline, but you'll settle for quiet. Silence conquers all.

The bedroom is a problematic banishment site because that's where all your kid's toys are. Don't let that stop you.

Seriously, where else would you send your child? The kitchen has food, the living room has the TV, and the bathroom is your sanctuary. It's bad enough that they occasionally defile it with their presence. Don't let them move in there.

To stop your kid from playing while they're in trouble, tell them to stay on their bed. For an adult, this would be the ultimate reward. For a kid, it's capital punishment. Admittedly, if you don't check on them, they'll just sneak off their bed to play with all their cool stuff. Let them. They won't want to get caught, so they'll play quietly. Mission accomplished.

The Best Places to Exile Your Kid

Location	Pro	Con
Their Room	They might finally play with all those expensive toys you bought them.	They'll still say they're bored.
Your Room	It's away from the main living area.	They'll snoop around. Make sure that one drawer is locked.
The Basement	They'll survive tornadoes.	You won't.
The Garage	They'll be isolated.	That's how this whole mess started.
The Yard	You won't see them.	Your neighbors will.
The Streets	They can say they grew up there.	They'll never stop saying it.

| Another Country | It's total banishment. | It requires six months of planning for a passport. |
| The Moon | In space, no one can hear you whine. | Transportation may be pricey. |

Grounded

If sending your kid away won't work, keep them close instead. In the traditional form of grounding, you keep your kid home, allowing them to leave only for a job or school. It's like work release from prison, only your kid doesn't have an ankle monitor. Those cost extra.

The downsides of grounding are obvious. If your kid is being awful, the last thing you want is to keep them around. You're the one who's really being punished. Your kid may recognize this and act out. Do you have the resolve to outlast them? You're a bare minimum parent. The answer is no.

Rather than keeping your child with you, you could ground them from something other than leaving the house, like screen time. Last chapter, you saw the extensive benefits of letting your kid glue themselves to the TV. Banning them from it will hurt your kid, but it will hurt you more. They'll hover around you, sighing heavily to express their despair. But no matter how much they complain, being grounded won't kill them—even if, after a while, you wish it would. At least then the whining would stop.

If your kid doesn't like TV shows or video games, you can still ground them, but you'll have to get creative. For introverted children who love learning, the only meaningful things you can

199

ban them from are books. Though if that's your kid's only interest, it raises the question of how they got grounded in the first place. Maybe they read disrespectfully. You can see it in their eye movements. If you have to ground your kids from books, you're doing a good job as a parent. Too good. Make your kid watch TV or something. Nobody likes a showoff.

Top Things to Ground Your Kid From

What's Banned	Pro	Con
Riding Bikes	Can't speed off to cause trouble.	Will cause trouble at home.
Dessert	There's more for you.	There will be more of you.
A Favorite Toy	You'll have a valuable hostage.	Your kid might stage a rescue. Hide the grappling hooks.
TV	You can watch whatever you want.	While you're distracted, your kid could find other garages.
Their Phone	Your kid will stop talking to their friends.	They'll start talking to you.
Sports	You won't have to drive them to practices and games.	Your kid will drive you insane.

Music	You won't have to listen to it blasting through the house.	Your kid will sing it to you instead.
Friends	It cuts off access to troublemakers.	Your kid is trouble incarnate.

Hard Labor

If you're motivated—which you aren't—you can punish your kid with extra chores. The problem is that chores are things that need to be done. If you punish your kid by making them do the laundry, you're really punishing yourself by forcing your family to wear poorly washed clothes. Have fun looking homeless.

There aren't any important chores you can trust a child to do well. In fact, not doing chores might be what you grounded them for in the first place. If you make them redo the chores they neglected, your clothes won't just be dirty; they'll be burning in a ditch. This chapter has more fire than I expected. Kids are terrifying.

Public Humiliation

The downside of punishing your kid by putting them in time-out or grounding them from their tablet is that it won't earn you any praise from other adults. If loose acquaintances can't validate your parenting decisions, what's the point?

Enter public humiliation. Instead of addressing the problem in a mature and thoughtful manner, some parents make their kid wear a humiliating sign and stand on a street corner to show the world. Of course, the world in this case is just a few hundred cars traveling by at high speeds. Passing motorists won't teach your kid a lesson. Drivers hate two things: reading and helping.

The real impact of sign shaming only hits home once you post the pictures online. That's when millions of stationary people will have a chance to read the sign and appreciate your parenting brilliance. Or tear you apart for being a terrible person. Either way, lots of people will see what you did, and that's the point. If you don't have an audience, did you even parent?

As a bare minimum parent, avoid this form of discipline at all costs. It's too much work. You have to drive to the store, buy posterboard, and write a message that's witty, succinct, and legible. Then you have to proofread the sign a thousand times to make sure there aren't any spelling errors. Otherwise you're the one being publicly humiliated.

Your child will experience enough humiliation in life without you piling on. In fact, too much shame could backfire. Your kid could be so humiliated that the experience vaccinates them against feeling shame for the rest of their life. Good luck stopping them then. They'll be invincible.

Listen Up

The biggest advantage you have over your child in the realm of discipline is your vocabulary. Use it. Explain to your kid what they did wrong and why it's unacceptable. Build an irrefutable argument. Gesticulate wildly. Include graphs and charts. Then sit back and watch your child ignore everything you just said.

Lectures as a form of discipline have numerous advantages. Effectiveness isn't one of them.

The upside of being ignored is you won't have to think of a new lecture each time. No matter how many times you repeat yourself, your kid won't hear a word you say. You'll always have a fresh audience. And if all forms of discipline are equally ineffective, you might as well do the one that's easiest for you. Saying things is easier than doing them. Plus it gives you the moral authority to say "I told you so" when your kid screws up. Then their mistakes are their fault, not yours. Deflecting blame is a hallmark of good parenting.

What Lecture Clichés Really Mean

Phrase	Meaning
Grow up.	Be dead inside like me.
When I was your age . . .	I don't remember anything from back then, but here's a morality tale I made up.
I hate repeating myself.	But that won't stop me.
You're better than this.	We both know you aren't.
I'm disappointed in you.	You can't disappoint me. My expectations are too low.
What don't you understand?	You understand. You're just a jerk.
We'll get through this together.	If I left you on someone's doorstep, they'd give you back.
I love you.	I wish you were a puppy.

The Disappointed Sigh

Legend has it that some parents can stop their child dead in their tracks simply by exhaling. With a single sigh, these Jedi of child-rearing can make their kid feel overwhelmed with guilt. As a parent, you carry that feeling every second of every day. Let your kid carry your emotional baggage for a while.

For a disappointed sigh to teach your child a lesson, your kid has to care what you think of them. If you figure out how to make that happen, let me know. Also, you have to forgo all other disciplinary techniques. You can't banish your child to their room and then sigh. Your kid won't hear you huffing three rooms away.

Sorry, Not Sorry

The discipline methods I've outlined here might not work, but that doesn't mean you've failed. The only way you can truly strike out as a bare minimum parent is if you don't discipline your child at all. Unless you try too hard. That always means you lose.

The most likely disciplinary outcome is that your kid will pretend to be sorry. Eventually, your child will answer to someone with real power—a manager, a judge, a mafia godfather who makes them an offer they can't refuse—and that feigned remorse could save their life. Your seemingly futile disciplinary efforts might turn your child into a functional employee or prevent them from going to jail or getting whacked. By at least attempting to discipline them, you're teaching them vital survival skills they can use for the rest of their life. If you do that, they can't blame you for anything. Well, they can, but they shouldn't.

Of course, it's possible discipline isn't your child's problem at all. Maybe they're not a monster. Maybe they're just hungry. Preheat the oven. It's time to give your kid something else to complain about.

Chapter 15

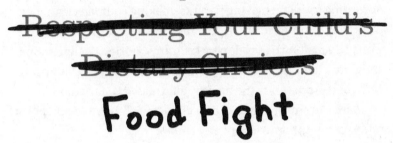

~~Respecting Your Child's Dietary Choices~~

Food Fight

Food is great. Unless you're a young child. Then it falls somewhere between an inconvenience and outright torture. Before puberty, kids resist food like adults resist exercise. Not all foods, of course. Children make exceptions for anything covered in cheese, ketchup, or chocolate. Those aren't toppings; they're the elixirs of life.

Nobody knows why young kids are such picky eaters. Your child loves and trusts you above all others, yet they also suspect you're trying to poison them. It's a valid concern if you've ever tasted brussels sprouts.

But in trying to protect themselves from dangerous foods, your kid does more harm than good. Not to get too technical, but if your child doesn't eat, they'll contract a medical condition called death. As a bare minimum parent, you should avoid that diagnosis for your kid at all costs. It's less work to keep an existing kid alive than to start over with a new one.

Against the Multigrain

Believe it or not, making sure your kid eats is controversial. According to overachieving parents, making your kid clean their plate will traumatize them for life. Never mind that their life won't be very long if they don't take in any calories. Uptight moms and dads claim forced eating creates an unhealthy relationship with food. Apparently the healthy alternative is starvation.

Bare minimum parents don't buy any of that. We don't buy much of anything. We're pretty cheap.

Young children are motivated more by taste than by hunger. A kid could eat candy until their stomach literally explodes. The sudden combustion would just create more room. But if the same kid had a choice between starvation and eating a single stalk of broccoli, they'd walk toward the light. There are no vegetables in heaven.

There are three times a day a young child is guaranteed not to be hungry, and those are breakfast, lunch, and dinner. Their appetite will return as soon as you clear the table. You might try to capitalize on that by cooking a new meal or pulling out the secret reserve meal you set aside for just this occasion. Don't bother. It would just make your kid lose their appetite again. The more time you spend preparing something, the less likely your kid is to eat it. Your effort is the world's most powerful diet plan. Get used to it.

Skipping one meal should make your kid hungrier for the next, but it won't. Your child has the willpower to resist an infinite number of breakfasts, lunches, and dinners. In between meals, they'll complain they want snacks without making the connection that they wouldn't be hungry if they ate the food you literally put in front of them three times a day. Instead, they'll skip meal after meal until they fade out of existence or you finally give them what they want. Chocolate chip cookies are cheaper than a funeral.

Gird Your Tenderloins

So you should just feed them whatever they want, right? Not even close. Though it seems like the easy thing to do, surrendering to your child's culinary whims will make your life infinitely harder. Once your child understands they own you, their demands will only increase. Soon, instead of snacking on chocolate chip cookies, they'll brush their teeth with them. Don't even ask about the mouthwash.

As a bare minimum parent, you should stand your ground on meals. "I'm full" is always a lie. Your kid will find more room as soon as you bring out dessert. A child's stomach is big enough to hold two tablespoons of mashed potatoes or forty pounds of taffy. Fifty if it's saltwater.

This selective space allotment is deliberate. Your child will find one or two foods they like and never make room for anything else. Once they eat macaroni and cheese, there's no reason to try other foods. You can't top perfection.

Don't empower this slow suicide. You're an adult—allegedly. Make your kid eat the meal you made. If it's good enough for you, it's good enough for the person you created in your image and likeness. You'll have a hard time proving it, though, because your kid won't want to let it hit their tongue. They'll know they don't like it just by squinting at it from across the room.

Too Much of a Good Thing

As long as your kid is actively ingesting food, you've done the bare minimum. Don't worry about the side effects. The experts that overachieving parents listen to are terrified of childhood obesity, but they shouldn't be. It's hard enough to get your kid to eat anything. If your child gains too much weight, you're parenting right. The experts are just mad your kid would out-last theirs in a famine.

Things That Are Your Fault
According to Parenting Experts

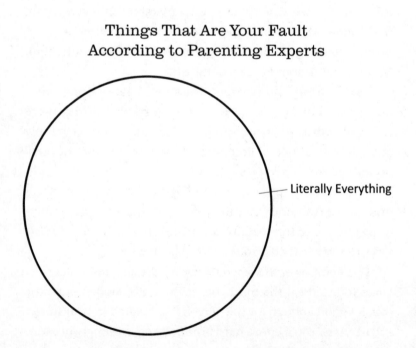

Literally Everything

A child's metabolism is a magical thing. It turns on and off at random. One day, your kid will eat their body weight in a single sitting, and the next, they'll be on pace to take one bite a year. It all depends on your child's age, the phase of the moon, and whether or not you offered them ice cream. There's no way to know if your kid really doesn't need food at the moment or if they've simply chosen to fade out of existence. Anything beats meatloaf night.

It's better to err on the side of too much food than not enough. One way you end up with a large child, and the other way you get a dead one. Use any means necessary to get your kid to finish their food. If they hate you for it later in life, at least they'll still be alive. The dead don't hold grudges. Except when they do, but that's a problem for the exorcists.

Besides, if your kid ends up fat, it won't be because you made them finish a peanut butter sandwich when they were five. Experts only think that's a threat because experts are paid to find threats. Without imaginary dangers, they'd be out of a job. And then their kids wouldn't have anything to eat.

Regardless of whether or not you make your kid clean their plate, nobody has a good relationship with food. It's a testament to our dominance as a species that our greatest danger is being too well fed. We're victims of our own success. That triple fudge sundae isn't a dessert; it's a victory lap. Eat up.

Eat It or Else

Making your kid eat takes balance. You don't want your child to starve, but you also don't want to violate your bare minimum principles. There's no point in living if you have to work for it.

Fear not—you can coerce your kid into eating AND be lazy. Mix and match these tactics until your child finishes their dinner or grows up and moves out, whichever comes first.

- *The Waiting Game*: Order your child to sit at the table until their food is gone. Make sure you don't have anywhere else to be that month.

- *Positive Reinforcement*: Praise your kid every time they take a bite. Get loud. Use pom-poms and a megaphone. Deploy streamers. They'll eat faster to end the embarrassment. Be ready with the Heimlich maneuver.

- *The Numbers Game*: Tell your kid they can be done after a certain number of bites. Quibble over the amount of food that constitutes a bite. Use third-party negotiators as necessary. With luck, your kid will focus more on the numbers than on their food. They won't even notice they've cleaned their plate—or they'll avoid eating anything, but become good at math. Either way, you win.

- *Half-Off Sale*: Give your kid twice as much food as normal, then tell them they only have to eat 50 percent of it. They'll feel like they got a deal. If it's good enough for a used car salesman, it's good enough for you.

- *Rebranding*: Serve the same foods as always but call them something different. Chicken breasts are "mega chicken nuggets," and mashed potatoes are "shredded French fries." If your kid doesn't believe you, apply ketchup. Then it will all taste the same anyway.

- *Temptation Island*: Tell your kid that if they finish their dinner, they'll get an awesome dessert. Then bring it out and eat it in front of them. They still won't finish their meal, but at least you won't have to share.
- *Transfiguration*: Make sound effects to turn a spoon or fork into a plane, train, or other inedible form of transportation. Your kid will want to put it in their mouth. Deep down, every child is a mini Godzilla.
- *The Hunger Games*: Tell your kid if they wait too long, you'll eat their food. They won't race you. In fact, they'll probably want you to eat it. But at least you can blame your extra pounds on them. Baby weight only gets worse after they're born.

If any of these tactics work for you, let me know. I'm still trying the waiting game. My kids have been at the table so long, I had time to write this book.

Special Selection

Don't beat yourself up if the meals you make for your kid don't hit every category on the food pyramid. Even if you try to feed your kid the healthiest foods possible, you won't be able to. Nutritional science changes all the time. Within your own lifetime, you've seen foods go from bad for you to good for you to bad for you again. If you feed your kid too much fat when fat is good and it suddenly becomes bad, you poisoned your child. But if you deliberately poison your child, you might accidentally make them healthier. It's best to feed your kid a wide variety of foods. That way the stuff that helps them and the stuff that kills them will cancel out.

Enforce that variety, no matter how hard your kid resists. It's dangerous to give your child a special menu they don't need. When you let your kid out of eating something one time, you take it off the menu forever. Showing weakness in front of a child is like bleeding in front of a shark. The only thing on the menu will be you.

Your child won't eat the same two or three foods forever. Their tastes will broaden as they age and will go into overdrive once they move out. It's amazing how good everything tastes when you mix hunger with poverty.

By forcing your kid to clean their plate when they're young, you'll hit all three benchmarks of successful parenting without breaking a sweat. If you teach your child to eat when there's food, not when they feel like it, they're more likely to survive when they move out and have to support themselves. Those doughnuts in the break room aren't a snack; they're a free meal. Your kid is also less likely to be a social deviant if you break them of their arbitrary dietary restrictions at an early age. If they grow up and insist on eating a specialty diet like organic or gluten-free, they'll have to rob a bank just to cover the grocery bill. Finally, even if you do wreck your kid's eating habits by feeding them when they don't want to eat, they won't blame you for their weight when they're an adult. They'll just look back wistfully on a time when they didn't have to cook for themselves.

But until then, it'll be up to you to make your kid eat enough to stay alive. Don't be shamed by overachieving parents. In the long run, your kid won't hate you for making them clean their plate. Their only regret will be not eating more when they had the chance. A metabolism is a terrible thing to waste.

Chapter 16
Dressing Your Child
for ~~Success~~
Survival

If your kid eats, they'll grow. And if they grow, they'll go through clothes. A lot of them.

Clothes matter. To overachieving parents, they're important because they make a powerful statement about who you are and where you fit into society. To bare minimum parents, they're important because they stop you from being naked. And the world is grateful.

Not that there's anything wrong with the human body. It just isn't made to withstand the extreme conditions of the environment. Exposed flesh won't last long in the Arizona summer or the Canadian winter. Honestly, Canada isn't suitable for human life in general, but that's another story. This story is about how being naked has consequences. It's how you ended up with a kid in the first place.

As a bare minimum parent, you must dress your child to comply with public nudity laws and to keep your kid safe. Think of your child's outfit less as a fashion statement and more as personalized body armor. Use it to help them withstand hostile environments like the desert or the classroom. In both cases, the goal is to stay cool. It's survival of the hippest.

The Message Clothes Send about Your Kid

Clothing	What It Says about Your Kid
Ascot	They know what an ascot is.
Turtleneck	They're hiding a vampire bite.
Shoes Named after a Famous Basketball Player	They spent their life savings on shoes named after a famous basketball player.
Tie	They're attending a function against their will.
Fur Coat	They're haunted by fox ghosts.
Pocket Protector	They work at NASA in the 1960s.
Suspenders	They've never heard of belts.
Cape	They're going to live with you for a long time.

Hidden in Plain Sight

In a social environment, clothes can protect your child in two ways: by helping them fit in or by making them stand out. Fitting in is less work because you can just copy the other kids.

As a bare minimum parent, you should obviously lean toward fashion plagiarism.

In popular culture, fitting in is portrayed as a bad thing. Kids who dress alike are called sheep. That's insulting to people and barnyard animals alike. Humans can't tell sheep apart, but to a sheep, other sheep each look unique. At least I assume they do. Full disclosure: When preparing for this book, I didn't interview any livestock.

Blending in with the crowd offers certain protections. Schools of fish clump together in huge, indistinguishable crowds to confuse predators, which are unable to pick a target and thus miss them all. It's kind of like when you can't make up your mind at an all-you-can-eat buffet, so you just stand there indecisively until you collapse from hunger. And that's why I don't go out to eat anymore.

Blending in with the crowd works just as well for your kid. Dress them no better and no worse than their peers. When it comes to camouflage, nothing beats uniform mediocrity. Fading into the background will help your kid dodge unrealistically high expectations from teachers and coaches. Your child can't fly too close to the sun if they spend all day lounging in the shade.

That's not the only attention your child will escape. Bullies can't single out your kid if your child is exactly as unremarkable as everybody else's. It's impossible for mean kids to insult your child without also insulting every other kid just like them. A lone bully is no match for a mob.

Still, dressing your child like everybody else has its drawbacks. When kids dress too much alike, children zero in on minor differences. Maybe your kid's polo shirt isn't quite the right shade of blue or their pants have pleats. Or don't have pleats. I forget which is bad, but it'll probably change a few times before the printing of this book.

The camouflage of the herd is only worth it if it makes life easier. If it causes problems, protect your child by making them stand out.

Creatures That Hide in Crowds

Creature	How It Works
Tuna	Densely pack themselves into metal cans for protection.
Zebras	Stripes drive away predators by offending their fashion sense.
Wildebeests	Splash all the water out when they cross rivers, causing alligators to dehydrate.
American Bison	Use their superior numbers to run hunters out of bullets—unsuccessfully.
Crows	Nothing wants to eat them anyway. They just like being creepy together.
Unicorns	They didn't swarm well enough. Now they're all gone.
Kids	When they cluster together, adults back away.
Adults	Hide behind coworkers until the boss picks another "volunteer" for that big project.

Standing Out

In nature, animals use bright colors to attract mates or ward off enemies. Birds do it, so you know it's a good idea. They used to be dinosaurs.

Your kid's situation is different because they don't have plumage. Probably. If they do, consult a doctor. But even without feathers, your kid can still employ nature's basic color tactics. Dress them in something eye-catching. The more sequins and rhinestones, the better. With any luck, your child will reflect enough sunlight to blind people. Then it won't matter what they wear.

The drawback is anyone who isn't blinded will continue staring at your kid. Your child will need self-confidence to pull it off. They'll either rise to the occasion or be crushed by it. Grab some popcorn. This should be fun.

Clothes That Make Your Kid Stand Out

Clothing	Pro	Con
Elvis Outfit	Instantly recognizable.	Increases odds of being abducted by aliens.
Inflatable T-rex Costume	No one can look away from those tiny inflatable arms.	Thwarted by standard-sized doorways.

Clothing	Pro	Con
T-shirt with a Funny Saying	Your kid gets to be witty without the work.	Loses its impact when worn for the hundredth time.
Bright Orange	They'll be safe during hunting season.	Might accidentally get drafted as a traffic cone.
Chainmail	Effective against bullies.	Ineffective against longbows.
Life Jacket	Ready if a water main breaks and floods the school.	Will be the top suspect if a water main breaks and floods the school.
Heart on Their Sleeve	Lets everyone know how they feel.	The heart works best inside the body.
A Padded Suit Used to Train Attack Dogs	Safe from attack dogs.	Vulnerable to being stuck on their back like a turtle.

Clothing Categories

Contrary to what overachieving parents believe, you don't need hundreds of different outfits to make your kid blend in or stand out. That's a lot of money—and a lot of laundry. You might think kids will only go through one set of clothes a day regardless of what's in their closet, but that's not how clothes work. The more options your kid has, the more disposable their clothes will seem, and the harder your kid will be on them. They can wear their dump truck shirt AND their dinosaur shirt in the same day if they pry open that can of house paint. There's no such thing as childproof.

As a bare minimum parent, your life will be simpler and less consumed by laundry if you give your kid just a handful of outfits in a few different categories. Clothes are like silverware. You don't need eight specialized spoons to eat a meal when each one is basically a mini food shovel. You'd be fine with just a spoon, a fork, and a knife—as long as you're not eating at a gunfight. Similarly, you can dress your kid properly with just three types of clothes: good clothes, school clothes, and everyday clothes. You only need enough of each type to get your kid through a week or two. Less than that and you'll have to constantly run the washing machine; more than that and you'll have mountains of extra laundry to wash when you finally get to it. Basically, there's no escaping laundry, but with too many outfits, your child will reek of effort. Nobody wants to raise the smelly kid.

Maybe you think three types of clothing seem excessive for a bare minimum parent. Couldn't your kid get away with two types, or maybe just one? Everybody looks good in a jumpsuit.

Well, not everybody. Really just pilots and inmates. For everyone else, three kinds of clothes is the fewest you need to awkwardly scrape by in any social situation. Any less than that and your kid will have to show up places dressed wrong or not dressed at all. To avoid blame, you have to keep your kid covered, literally and metaphorically. Stick with these three types of clothes and you can't go wrong. Well, you could, but you'd have to work at it.

Good Clothes

These clothes are too nice to play in, so guess what your child will do. The nicer the outfit, the more likely a kid is to wear it while rolling down a hill. The best grass stains are 360 degrees.

Dress clothes are like a formal living room: too nice to use and a burden to keep clean. They're the least functional part of your child's wardrobe AND the most expensive, so keep your good clothing purchases to a minimum. Unfortunately, you can't avoid good clothes completely. At least a few of the pictures on your wall must show your kid in formal attire. This will prove your kid achieved whatever religious or educational milestone was on the agenda for that day. When your kid grows up, they'll thank you for making them dress so nicely. Just kidding. All they'll remember is how hot and miserable they were. And then they'll turn around and put their own kid through the same ordeal. Misery is a family tradition.

School Clothes

Schools are unique because they have the law on their side. Your kid has to go to school and follow the rules that come with it. That includes the dress code. You'll either be forced to buy clothes that comply with the school's standards or withdraw your kid and homeschool. You win this round, institutionalized education.

School clothes aren't as nice as good clothes, but they're more functional. As a parent, you don't want to spend too much on these outfits because at some point your kid will play in them—at least before schools abolish recess in favor of more cram sessions for standardized tests. It still counts as exercise if your kid fills in enough circles.

Your job as a bare minimum parent is to dress your kid so they won't get sent home. Every day your child isn't returned to you early is a victory. The free time you gain is worth the price of a new wardrobe.

Everyday Clothes

This is where standards go to die. At home, far from the judgmental eyes of people who might report your kids to child protective services, you can dress your kid however you want. Say good-bye to the cruel oppression of buttons, snaps, and zippers. Say hello to the sweet liberation of elastic waistbands and stretchy fabrics. In these loose, comfortable clothes, your child will have total freedom of movement. But they'll be at home, so they won't move at all.

Not all everyday clothes are created equal. There are the ones your kid can wear to the grocery store because they still look presentable if you're far away and have bad eyesight. Then there are the clothes your kid can only wear around the house because they're dirty and torn up but still cover the necessary areas. Finally, there are clothes they can barely even wear around the house. These are a step away from being turned into rags. Don't bother washing them. That only makes the stains stronger. Keep everyday clothes of each type on hand so your kid is ready for every level of idleness. There's nothing worse than slacking off unprepared.

Most everyday clothes are made, not bought. They start their existence as school clothes and get downgraded after a hard life. People aren't the only things that fall apart as they age. Everyday clothes seldom start out as good clothes, though. Nobody plays tag in an old First Communion dress. Though maybe they should. At least then your kid would get to wear it twice.

Back to Basics

If you treat clothes as tools for physical and social survival rather than as fashion statements, you can hit all three benchmarks of successful parenting with minimal effort. Your child will more easily support themselves in the workforce if they know how to blend in to avoid work or how to stand out to steal credit. All it takes is the right ugly sweater. If your child is clothed, they won't be arrested for being naked in public, so you can cross at least one type of social deviant off the list. And if your kid tries to blame you for their problems based on how you dress them, you could always suggest they buy their own clothes. That'll shut them up quick.

Make all clothing decisions for your kid with those benchmarks in mind. If you do it right for your oldest child—with minimal thought and even less effort—you'll never have to do it again. Sorry, every kid after the first one. Enjoy your hand-me-downs.

Chapter 17

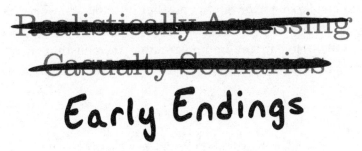

~~Realistically Assessing Casualty Scenarios~~

Early Endings

I have some bad news for you: Your child is going to die.

    I mean, not immediately. I don't know your kid, so I can't diagnose them one way or the other. They're probably safe—for now.

    But someday your child will die, and you can't stop it. However, you can delay it for a while. This won't work forever, but it doesn't have to. You just want your child to outlive you. Odds are they will. Future advances in science combined with your own poor life choices mean they'll live longer than expected and you'll die long before you should. That seventy-five-year life span doesn't apply to people who have been through more eclipses than gym visits. Don't look up.

    Keeping your child alive long enough to outlive you is the most basic bare minimum parenting requirement. It's so basic, in fact, that I didn't even list it as one of the three main benchmarks of successful parenting. I suppose you could lump it under the one about your kid supporting themselves. It's hard for your child to hold down a job if they're dead, but they might have to anyway. Credit card debt follows you to hell.

To ensure your kid makes it, you'll be tempted to worry about every possible threat. Don't. There are more ways for your child to die than you can possibly imagine. But worrying about them won't do any good because it won't actually prevent them. In bare minimum parenting, the only thing more tragic than an early death is wasted effort. It takes courage to be lazy.

(Almost) Scared to Death

Telling a parent not to worry is like telling a fish not to swim. They don't even speak English. A threat to your kid is the fastest way to get your attention. Luckily, media organizations would never exploit this fear. Just kidding. Threats to your kid make up 90 percent of all broadcasts. The other 10 percent is sports.

You know these stories are a trick, but you can't look away. You want to know about every danger. The more unlikely, the better. You might ignore an article about exploding childhood diabetes rates, but you'll give your full attention to one about exploding waffles. Even though I made that up, you're still tempted to look into it. Just to be safe, give me all your waffles.

As nightly TV news has declined in popularity, the job of scaremongering has fallen to the internet, which gleefully added jet fuel to the dumpster fire. Now rather than having a handful of esteemed news anchors terrifying the public, there are millions of overachieving parents on the internet trying to out-horrify each other. Nothing goes viral like something new that could kill your child. Exploding waffles are so last month.

According to the hyper-protective moms and dads in cyberspace, the world is nothing but a chamber of horrors filled with increasingly unlikely ways your child can die. Think guinea pigs won't bite? Think again. They'll eat your kid's eyeballs. Baby-safe shampoo? Yeah, right. Three of its active ingredients are used in lethal injections. Bananas? More like mushy choke boomerangs. You better hope they come back when they get stuck in your kid's throat.

Scary articles are everywhere because they're easy to write. Technically everything can kill your child. Look at any random object near your kid. Surprise, it's a death trap. A living room lamp, for example, could take out your child in more ways than a trained warrior monk: electrocution by bad wiring, strangulation by the power cord, or laceration by broken glass. You can go through this mental process with anything in your house. Even stashing your kid in a plastic bubble won't protect them, since it would act as a giant magnifying glass. At least the ants would have their revenge.

Deadliest Things in Your House

Object	Danger It Poses
TV	It can fall down and fatally wound your child or your wallet.
Knives	A child can sense them through closed drawers and solid walls.

Object	Danger It Poses
Power Outlets	They might shock your child and drive up your electric bill.
Chemicals under the Sink	A child is a thousand times more likely to drink them than anything you put in their sippy cup.
Bathtubs	They're drowning hazards if you're small or drunk.
Power Tools	There's nothing scarier than a toddler with a welding torch.
The Mirror	It kills your self-esteem.
Your Kid	They can turn anything into a weapon to hurt themselves or others.

The Real Threat

The dangers that actually kill people are the ones no one worries about because they don't show up on the news. The person who dies from a fluke gopher attack makes more headlines than the thousands of people who die from a common disease we should have eradicated by now. Then, instead of raising money to cure that disease, people will raise an army to fight the gophers. There's a reason we have bunker-busters.

Worrying about improbable causes of death won't save your child's life, but it could shorten your own. Your heart can only take so much stress. You have nothing to fear but fear itself, which could literally kill you.

Here are the causes of death you should never worry about:

1. *Anything in a lake*: Boating accidents, stagnant-water superviruses, and mythological loch monsters don't kill many people each year. Plus there's a treatment that's 100 percent effective against those fatalities. It's called "don't go in lakes."

2. *Wild animal attacks*: You're more likely to be killed by a family pet than by a random animal in nature. Unless your pet is a mountain lion. Then it's a toss-up.

3. *The latest scary teen trend*: Whether it's holding their breath till they pass out or pretending to be a plank of wood in dangerous places, most kids don't actually do that stuff. The few who do heard about it when their parents warned them not to do it. High schoolers are always on the lookout for fun new ways to acciden-tally kill themselves.

4. *Anything that involves foreign travel*: Nothing scares par-ents like an innocent kid dying in a strange place, but you have too many things to worry about in your own house to squeeze overseas dangers onto your radar. That gang of child abductors in the French Alps has much less relevance to your life than whether or not you put the lid on your pill bottle. The last thing you want is a toddler on Viagra.

Tread Carefully

While worrying is normally a waste of time worth avoid-ing, there is one point in a child's life when it can come in handy. When your child is between the ages of thirteen and nineteen, you should be afraid. Very afraid. Teenagers think they're invincible, so you have to do their worrying for them. Without you, they'd die before they learn it's a bad idea to go skinny-dipping at that haunted campground. At least they'll be a wiser ghost.

Teenagers are especially vulnerable to overlooking danger because they have adult bodies and reptile brains. You might think I'm exaggerating, but studies show high schoolers and crocodiles are equally susceptible to peer pressure. Not alligators, though. It's the only way to tell them apart.

The good news is your teen's "invincible" phase won't last forever. Eventually, they'll injure their way out of it. Teenagers are finally old enough that all their childhood cartilage has been replaced by bone. That means the aches and pains they accumulate now will last a lifetime. Gone are the days when they could somersault down a flight of stairs and spring back up like they meant to do that. They better stick the landing.

Pain is a great teacher. Worry about your kid until it hurts them to get out of bed. Then they'll be okay.

Rubber Kids

Until your kid becomes a teenager, it's okay to relax. It seems counterintuitive to worry less about little kids than big ones, but it really is the more efficient path. Small children always bounce back. Parents think of them as fragile flowers, but they're more like weeds: They show up whenever they want, grow like crazy, and make your yard look terrible. But most importantly, nothing kills them. I've seen dandelions soak up bottles of herbicide and toddlers eat handfuls of cereal from inside a dusty vent. Both pests are still here.

A bare minimum parent can't keep a small child safe twenty-four hours a day. Neither could a superhero. Unless they're also Bruce Wayne. Then they could pay their butler to do it. No matter how closely you watch them, your child will find dangers you never thought possible. If anyone can put themselves in mortal peril with a plunger, it's your kid. Maybe you'll arrive just in time to save the day, or maybe the situation will work itself out on its own. Every child on earth creates these crises on a daily basis, and most of them survive. So dial back the panic and wait for the second or third scream before you get out of your recliner. For once in your life, the odds are on your side. Don't blow it by parenting too hard.

Explaining Screams

Scream	Meaning	Appropriate Response
High and Shrill	Someone jumped out of the closet.	Stop jumping out of the closet.
Long and Drawn Out	A sibling stole their toy.	Don't get involved in civil wars.
Loud and Gurgly	They're having an underwater screaming contest.	Drain the bathtub.
Short and Quiet	They're trying to hide whatever they're up to.	Investigate immediately.

Scream	Meaning	Appropriate Response
Loud and Deep	They're pretending to be dinosaurs.	Stay away. They might attract real dinosaurs.
Oscillating Pitch	They're singing.	Invest in earplugs.
Wolf Howl	It's the full moon.	Lock your door.
Silence	Danger.	Run.

The Existential Threat

Keeping your child alive will help you meet the three bare minimum benchmarks of successful parenting. It's easier for your child to get a job and support themselves if they're still breathing. Likewise, your kid will be less of a social deviant if they're alive than if they're dead. Zombies seldom follow the rules. And as far as blame goes, your child can't be mad at you for NOT killing them. Even if you were certainly tempted from time to time.

Keeping your kid alive isn't that hard. I wouldn't have told you to do it if it were. As dangerous as the world is today, it's a lot safer than it used to be. But my advice on how to keep your child alive and turn them into a functional adult in the easiest way possible is just as effective today as it would have been in the past. Laziness is timeless. And I have the examples to prove it.

Chapter 18
Making History

^
Up

So far in this book, I've provided perfect, irrefutable advice on how to raise kids who are just as good or better than the children of overachieving parents with less effort from you. But I haven't shown you examples of how bare minimum parenting's principles worked out for people who followed them. Maybe "followed" isn't the right word since I'm just now writing them down. But some parents throughout history did what I would have told them to do anyway, so I'm retroactively claiming credit. It's not fair, but that won't stop me. Dead people can't sue.

It's challenging to use historical figures to prove bare minimum parenting works. If some long-dead person is still remembered today, they probably did something important. That exceeds the goals of bare minimum parenting. But the alternative is to use ordinary people no one has ever heard of, and that isn't ideal, either. It's tough to build a case based solely on Bill, the dairy manager at my local grocery store. Although I almost did anyway, not because I thought it would prove anything, but because I wanted free milk.

Instead, my examples in this chapter are Abraham Lincoln and Joseph Stalin. No other book has compared these two men based on how their parents raised them—or based on anything at all. They lived at different times and had nothing to do with each other. This research is as cutting edge as it is pointless. So it's exactly like everything else in academia.

Some of what I'm about to say might sound controversial. And by "controversial" I mean "wildly inaccurate." But who's to say what's a lie and what's a slightly smaller lie? Nobody can go back in time to prove what really happened, and if they could, they would alter history, so it wouldn't count. This was proven by a scientific source called every time travel movie ever. Look at that, I'm even citing my work.

And really, even the experts don't know what happened back then. There are thousands of years of history where the only primary source is a single, partially burned scroll. Historians assume that scroll is the definitive work of literature for that civilization, but maybe the reason it was burned in the first place was because it sucked. That's like future historians concluding this book was important because someone tried to flush it down the toilet.

If the facts I present here don't jive with what you've read elsewhere, that doesn't mean someone (specifically, me) is lying. It just means I'm having a scholarly disagreement with the other experts. My research is just as valid as theirs, as long as their research also consisted entirely of looking up Lincoln and Stalin on Wikipedia. Countless teachers have told me that isn't a real source. But to be fair, this isn't a real book.

Before we go any further, it's important for you to under-stand my historical biases. I grew up in the Midwest, where Lincoln spent most of his life. Multiple states claim him: Ken-tucky, where he was born; Indiana, where he spent his child-hood; Illinois, where he practiced law; and Ohio, which he passed through on his way to better states. The term "Mid-west" just refers to the loose collection of states that act like Lincoln belongs to them. Feelings about it are pretty strong. It almost started a second civil war.

In my neck of the woods, Honest Abe is as close as you can come to a god. If Jesus and Lincoln both came back from heaven and arrived in the Midwest on the same day, there would be a line around the block to see Lincoln and no line at all to see Jesus, mainly because Jesus would be in line to see Lincoln, too. Clearly, I like the guy a little bit. But I promise to be impartial when comparing him to Stalin, who everyone agrees was a repulsive monster with no redeeming qualities.

Lincoln vs. Stalin

	Lincoln	Stalin
Height	Six feet, four inches.	Shorter than Lincoln.
Weight	Ten bald eagles.	Some weird metric measurement.
Arm Span	Long enough to hug all of America.	Too short to push the launch button.

	Lincoln	Stalin
How They Made the World a Better Place	Won the Civil War and freed the slaves.	Died.

Honestly the Best

Abraham Lincoln was born in the early 1800s, the son of a mother and a father. His parents had names, which you're welcome to look up on your own. The important thing isn't who they were, but how they raised their kids. They were bare minimum parents by the modern definition, but back then they were just called parents. Simply surviving took considerable effort, so parents didn't have much energy left for anything else. Nobody parent-shamed anyone about it, though, because they were all too busy trying not to die of tuberculosis themselves. It's harder than it sounds.

According to historical records, Abraham Lincoln's mom and dad never attended a single youth soccer game. Abe didn't care because he didn't play organized sports. Also, soccer didn't exist in America back then. George Washington won a war to keep it out.

The only activity Lincoln did for sure was survive. It was challenging because at least one of his childhood homes only had three sides. The next time you feel like a bad parent, remember the mother and father of America's greatest president couldn't even give him the bare minimum number of walls.

As hard as it was to stay alive, Lincoln was better at it than the rest of his family. His mother died after a brief illness when Lincoln was still a kid. Historians disagree on the cause of

Number of Soccer Games Attended by the Parents of Famous Historical Figures

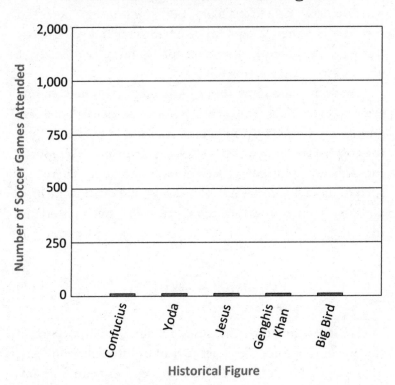

death, but it's notable that she was survived by other moms in houses with four walls.

Undeterred, Lincoln's dad remarried within a year. Relationships moved faster back then because people could die at any moment. You never knew if a first date would be followed by a second date or a funeral.

Lincoln gained some step-siblings through his new step-mom. If this story sounds familiar, it's because it's the basis for *The Brady Bunch.* I forget the name of the kid who was supposed to be Lincoln, but it was the ugly one. The big, quirky family then moved from Kentucky to Indiana and finally to Illinois, where Lincoln helped his dad set up a new farm. There's no record of whether Abe got his own bedroom, but you can bet this time the house had an appropriate number of walls. It saved a ton on the heating bill.

That's the bare minimum childhood Lincoln had, and he grew up to be Abraham Lincoln. Before you try harder at parenting, ask yourself if you expect your kid to be better than the greatest leader in world history. If you do, never set foot in the Midwest or you'll be chased out for blasphemy. There's no such thing as "better than Lincoln." Your kid can only tie him, and even then, only if they're his clone. Get them tested just in case.

Stallin' for Stalin

Then there's the other guy: Joseph Stalin, brutal dictator of the Soviet Union for three decades of uninterrupted misery. There are a few key differences between Lincoln and Stalin. First of all, unlike Lincoln, Stalin is not beloved by people in the Midwest. He's not beloved by people anywhere. Except maybe aging communists in Russia who Stalin didn't get around to killing. There are only so many hours in a day. Again, my bias might be showing here, but based on the body count he racked up among his own countrymen, Stalin is one of the worst people ever to live. Though in his defense, he did beat Hitler and had a great mustache, so maybe it's a wash.

I'm not here to judge historical figures by their facial hair. (If I were, that award would go to Lincoln.) I'm here to judge their childhoods by bare minimum parenting standards. On that scale, Stalin stands a better chance. If there's one place that excels at having the bare minimum of everything, it's Russia.

Like Lincoln, Stalin had a subpar childhood. He was born in Georgia roughly a decade after Lincoln died. Not the Georgia that surrendered in terror when Lincoln flexed his biceps, but the one in the Russian Empire. Tough break.

As if the disappointment of not living in America wasn't bad enough, Stalin's father drank too much. He overachieved at being Russian, and it killed him. At least he died doing what he loved.

Undeterred, Stalin's mom worked multiple side jobs and called in favors from a priest to get her son into a religious school, a coveted spot in a country where simply not freezing to death was considered an accomplishment. Stalin was the first one in his family to receive a formal education, a major victory for his overachieving mother. He made the most of the opportunity. Just kidding. He dropped out, became an atheist, and ruled the Soviet Union with an iron fist. I might have skipped a few steps in there, but you get the idea.

So is Stalin a success story or a cautionary tale? Let's just say no one wants their kid to grow up to be the next Stalin. He killed millions of Nazis with his army and millions of his own people with his incompetence. In the end, he was as bad at keeping people alive as his mom was at doing the bare minimum. Oops.

Thanks to his questionable upbringing, Stalin missed two-thirds of the benchmarks of successful parenting. He turned out to be a social deviant, and he can definitely blame his parents for it. Secret political murders aren't the hallmark

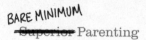
of a well-adjusted human being. If you must be a murderer, at least be open about it. Take some pride in your work.

Stalin's mom did manage to hit one successful parenting benchmark: She made Stalin self-sufficient. According to historical records, adult Stalin never called his mom to ask for money. Although she may have been dead by then. It's hard to say. I'd have to Google it.

Stalin could take care of himself, but his mom broke the bare minimum code to get him to that point. She used dirty tricks like hard work and networking to get Stalin an education. That's the modern equivalent of ruthlessly doing whatever it takes to get your kid into a top-tier daycare. Stalin in turn learned to mercilessly pursue his own goals. In so doing, he decimated his own country and set in motion a Cold War that lasted half a century. Clearly overparenting turns children into maniacal despots. Well, it turned one child into a maniacal despot. In this chapter's sample size of two people, that's statistically significant.

Worst Parents in History

Parent	What They Did	Why It's Awful
Eve	Doomed mankind for an apple.	Not worth it for fruit. Maybe for bacon.
Abraham	Tried to sacrifice his child to God.	Ruined father–son bonding time forever.
Cinderella's Stepmother	Made Cinderella do all the chores.	Put perfectly capable servants out of work.

Godzilla	Too busy smashing buildings to raise his son.	Children with absentee fathers are more likely to grow up to be monsters.
Grendel's Mother	Gave birth to Grendel.	Set off a chain of events that forced generations of bored college students to read *Beowulf*.
The Mom in *Home Alone*	Forgot her kid in a different city twice.	Child Protective Services should have stepped in the first time.
Stalin's Dad	Drank too much.	Refused to share.
You	Nothing.	You're doing fine, but you're emotionally incapable of giving yourself a break.

Learning from the Great (and Not-So-Great)

What lessons should you take from the childhoods of Lincoln and Stalin? First and foremost, don't live in Russia. It's a land of cold and sadness, and nothing good ever comes from there. Unless this book ends up being available in Russian, in which case it's a cheerful land of prosperity and you should totally buy my guide.

Second, overachieving at parenting isn't just harder; it really is worse for your kid. Stalin's mom overachieved by doing everything possible to get her son into a good school, and it turned her kid into a supervillain. If she had chilled out a little, the world would have escaped the wrath of the Russian Lex Luthor. But she just had to impress her neighbors by pushing her son, and the price was nearly ending life as we know it in a nuclear holocaust. Well done.

Lincoln's parents, in contrast, were consistently minimalist. All of his guardians did the bare minimum to keep him alive. Lincoln was self-sufficient, wasn't a social deviant, and never blamed his parents for anything. If you want your kid to be like Lincoln and not like Stalin, be like Lincoln's parents. Other than the dying-young part. That's optional.

With that, it's time to wrap up this book—not because I've made my point, but because I've almost reached my contractually required word count. One more chapter should do the trick. I could write more, but that would be overachieving. I might not be the greatest childcare expert in the world, but at least I'm not a hypocrite.

Chapter 19
The Point of
~~Overachieving~~
No Return

You're not the first person to struggle as a parent. More than a hundred billion people have ever walked the earth, which is one hundred billion chances to get parenting right. Yet even after all that trial and error, there's no consensus on the right way to raise a child. You can't say the kids in an ancient civilization were any better or worse behaved than kids in modern times. In both cases, the children grew up, lived normal lives, and were forgotten. No matter how badly you screw up, people will get over it. It might just take a few centuries.

Yet the human race as a whole must be doing something right. We're not the ones on the verge of extinction. For all our flaws, we conquered the planet, and no other species is even close to taking it back. Some baby animals can run within minutes of being born and become self-sufficient adults in less than a year. Entire generations of mice can live and die before a human toddler learns to use the potty. But *Homo sapiens*, with offspring who are functionally useless for upward of eighteen years, in the end outperform every other member of the animal kingdom. Your child will continue this domination over all the creatures of the earth. You might not be a perfect parent, but evolution grades on a curve.

The truth is nobody knows the right way to raise a kid, not even your own parents. The people who brought you up felt just as lost and confused as you feel now. You turned out fine anyway. Or I assume you did. At the very least, you grew up to be literate and capable of affording this book. I'm willing to say as much in a letter of recommendation. Underwhelming employment, here you come.

Maybe you had the best parents in the world. Maybe you had mediocre parents. Or maybe you were literally raised by monsters. Freddy Krueger was a terrible neighbor, but that doesn't mean he couldn't be a good dad. But one way or another, those kids with good parents and those with bad parents and those with slasher-movie villain parents all grew up to be adequate if unremarkable adults. The people who raised you stressed out over nothing. In the end, mediocrity claims us all.

That's the real lesson of this book. Anyone who tells you that you're parenting wrong is wrong simply for assuming there's a right way at all. If your kid can support themselves, isn't a social deviant, and doesn't blame you for their problems, then you succeeded at parenting. Take a bow. You're no better or worse than average.

Amount of Knowledge Gained by Reading This Book

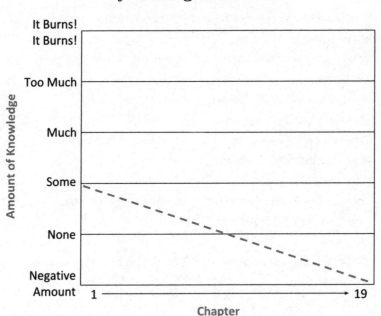

If you're an overachieving parent and you like that life-style, more power to you. Just don't feel like that's the only way. No matter how hard you work, your kid will turn out about the same as everybody else's. Bare minimum parents simply achieve averageness by the fastest route. If you want to take the longer, harder road, that's on you. The rest of us will try to save you some beer at the finish line. And by "try," I mean give you a half-hearted shrug when you ask why all the kegs are empty.

Pros and Cons of Finishing This Book

Pro	Con
You can now say you've read a parenting book.	It was written by me.
You don't have to read it anymore.	It can still haunt your dreams.
You realize you know more about parenting than I do.	No refunds.
Time you spent reading was time you didn't spend parenting.	Your house is now a pile of rubble.
You gave in and bought the book, so now I'll leave you alone.	I might write another one.
You can pass this book on to someone else.	You'll make a new enemy.

With that, you're officially a bare minimum parent. I'd give you a certificate, but printer ink is expensive. Instead, display this book in a place of prominence in your home, preferably next to whatever diploma you have. Finishing this book is more impressive than any degree, including an MD. Being a doctor teaches you to help other people, but only my guide helps the most important person in the world: me. Guess who can afford groceries this month.

I wish you the best of luck on your bare minimum parenting endeavors. Try to be lazier, but not too hard. And if you figure out a better way to raise a kid, I don't want to hear about it. Learning new things is too much work. Write your own shameless parenting guide.

Acknowledgments

This book didn't happen on its own. At the bare minimum, these are the people I should thank:

- My literary agent, Mark Gottlieb of Trident Media Group. I'm starting to wonder if there's a book proposal you can't sell. You need more of a challenge. I promise to make my next pitch considerably worse.
- Glenn Yeffeth, publisher of BenBella Books. You signed me for a second book before I sold a single copy of my first one. A wiser man might have hedged his bets. You doubled down. Thanks for betting big on me.
- Leah Wilson, BenBella editor-in-chief. If readers could see all the jokes you made me cut, I wouldn't have any readers left. Thanks for protecting me from me.
- My kids. You were the guinea pigs for the parenting techniques in this book. Thanks for not dying. That would have made the closing paragraphs super awkward.
- My wife. The internet only has to tolerate me in small bursts. You have to put up with me all the time. Thanks for not murdering me in my sleep.

About the Author

James Breakwell is a professional comedy writer and amateur father of four girls, ages eight and under. He is best known for his family-humor Twitter account @XplodingUnicorn, which boasts more than one million followers and has been featured on media outlets around the world. He also writes a parenting column for the *IndyStar*, where he antagonizes overachieving parents everywhere.

James's first book, *Only Dead on the Inside: A Parent's Guide to Surviving the Zombie Apocalypse*, has saved thousands of lives since its release in October 2017. To date, not a single person who's read it has died in a zombie attack. But if you do die, James will give you a refund. Offer null and void if you try to bite him.

Keep track of James's ongoing failings as a father and a human being at ExplodingUnicorn.com or on Facebook at www.Facebook.com/ExplodingUnicorn.

It's not easy being a parent these days.
There are bills to pay. Kids to feed.
And hordes of undead monsters to keep at bay.

JAMES BREAKWELL IS HERE TO HELP.

To learn more, visit:

EXPLODINGUNICORN.COM